MOUNT OF CONGREGATION

MARK A. DAVIS

Mount of Congregation

ISBN 978-1-940645-48-3

Cover photo: "We Clear the Way/The Corps of Engineers/United States Army" by Jes Wilhelm Schlaikjer. Courtesy of the George C. Marshall Foundation, Lexington, Virginia.

COURIER PUBLISHING

Greenville, South Carolina

PUBLISHED IN THE UNITED STATES OF AMERICA

FOR AUNT JUDY

ACKNOWLEDGEMENTS

Every family has a story. This was simply one of them. Special thanks to managing editor Butch Blume and the staff at Courier Publishing, who made this book possible; Jeffrey Kozak, director of library and archives, George C. Marshall Foundation, Lexington, Va.; the United States Holocaust Memorial Museum; Carol Steele, a true family historian; my family, including aunts, uncles and cousins, who took the time to share their memories; my wife, Melissa, for giving me the time, support and space to work on this project. Most of all, a very special thanks to the One from whom all blessings flow, Who still works behind the scenes to accomplish His will.

INTRODUCTION

It was finally time to take a break. Back then, I had my hands full with college and working as a nursing assistant on the medical surgical floor of our local hospital. While sitting down to have a quick bite to eat, my pager suddenly delivered a high-pitched, distinct alarm. At the same time, an announcement came over the hospital's intercom:

"Code blue ... ER ... Room 1A." Then again: "Code blue ... ER ... Room 1A."

Leaving my meal behind, I quickly made my exit from the ground floor and headed toward the stairs.

Being a member of the hospital's code team was a privilege in itself. I never thought I would have been part of such a group of talented individuals. Yet there I was, working with some of the best and brightest in the business. When they heard that I had been accepted to begin a physician assistant program in the upcoming fall semester, these caregivers and providers took me under their wing, exposing me to what I would soon encounter on an even more frequent basis. Needing all the experience I could get, especially in emergency situations, I eagerly accepted any duty when it came to patient care.

I avoided the elevator in situations like this, as time was of the essence. Knowing shortcuts was key to getting to a specific area of the hospital in the shortest amount of time, and I knew all of them. After all, my grandfather's construction company was the one that built the hospital when I was just a kid.

My own initial experience with the code team was performing

chest compressions on the patient who had no pulse — which, in my opinion, was actually the most strenuous part of the job, both physically and mentally. It's been said that the last face a patient sees before he or she dies is the face of the ER doctor working on them. In reality, I think it is instead those individuals performing cardiopulmonary resuscitation, who cannot help but make eye contact with the patient while performing CPR.

Many times patients were revived. Other times, no matter the length or breadth that the code team went to, there was no bringing them back.

Running up the stairs, I soon reached the first floor and saw other personnel of the code team entering the patient's room. It was orchestrated chaos as our training kicked in and, like second nature, we began to work on the patient. Orders were called out, and we soon confirmed that the patient in fact was in cardiac arrest — no pulse, and no breathing. CPR was initiated immediately.

Our emergency room doctor, who was already entering the patient's room along with the house supervisor nurse, took a look at the ECG monitor and immediately confirmed the patient was in ventricular fibrillation — V-fib — the most serious cardiac rhythm disturbance. It is when the heart quivers instead of pumping, due to disorganized electrical activity in the heart's ventricles.

The doctor grabbed and then placed the defibrillator paddles on the patient's chest.

"Clear!" he shouted.

We backed away from the patient as the doctor delivered the first electrical shock. Delivered through the chest wall, this initial shock momentarily stopped the heart's chaotic quivering, with the hope of allowing it to return to its normal rhythm.

As I stepped back, I suddenly recognized the patient's face. He was an older man who attended my grandfather's church. He had been exercising at the local gym that morning when he collapsed on the floor. He still had his exercise clothes and tennis shoes on when they brought him in.

The first jolt of electricity from the paddles was to no avail, as the ECG monitor demonstrated he was still in ventricular fibrillation. The paddles remained firmly against the patient's chest as the doctor charged the paddles to the next electrical level.

"Clear!" he commanded, as another shock was delivered.

Still in V-fib.

He again ordered, "Clear!" as a third shock was delivered at an even higher level of electricity.

But the patient was still in V-fib.

Orders were given, and we again approached the patient. The charge nurse placed a step stool for me to stand on. This was to help with the position I would be in while working above the patient. I resumed chest compressions. Medications were delivered through the IV, followed by another shock; then reassessment, and then the drug-shock, drug-shock sequence.

Each time, the ECG monitor was checked. The patient was still in V-fib.

Our code team worked with all its might to bring him back, but it was to no avail. After working through the entire ventricular fibrillation treatment algorithm, there was no change in the patient's condition. The doctor made the determination that efforts to restart his heart were futile and ordered an end to

CPR. In just a few moments, I had gone from taking a break in the cafeteria to responding to a code blue and witnessing someone I knew — a member of the aptly named "Greatest Generation" — being pronounced dead from cardiac arrest.

It was always sad to lose someone you were trying to help. The nurses began unhooking the equipment from the deceased patient as the ER doctor, accompanied by the house supervisor, went out to the waiting room to inform the family of their loss. The loved ones were devastated. Later, they came into the room to say their goodbyes.

After the family left, the charge nurse and I still had work to do, as we accompanied the body down the hallway and to the morgue. Hardly a word was spoken as we pulled the gurney into the mortuary.

I heard rumors that he was a veteran of World War II, which made me wonder about his family. Had they ever taken the time to record any of the stories and memories that made up the life of their grandfather? Did he ever share with his family personal experiences from that period in time? Was it recorded, or was it simply lost forever, now that he had died?

I had already begun researching my own grandfather's experience from World War II. He, too, had previously passed away from cardiac failure. He was also a member of the Greatest Generation and a veteran of the United States Army. I was privileged to grow up listening to him share, on rare occasions, some of what he had experienced as a soldier. As his grandchild, I felt inclined to compile an account, as complete as possible, about his experiences from the war, in order to share with future generations. His story is unique. The research I accumulated while in college — including family interviews, contacts with a few of his surviving fellow soldiers back in 2001, and an old family interview audiotape — only confirmed that inclination.

Unfortunately, with the passage of time, we have continued to lose these extraordinary members of our society. They are the ones who were brought up during the Great Depression and went on to fight and achieve victory in World War II, and they were the ones who sacrificed relentlessly on the home front whose contribution to the workforce made such a victory possible.

According to U.S. Department of Veterans Affairs statistics, only 558,000 of the 16 million Americans who served in World War II were alive in 2017. Within the next few years, they will all be gone.

My grandfather was a soldier in the Army's 42nd Infantry Division and was attached to the 142D (Combat) Engineer Battalion. The famous nickname for the 42nd Infantry Division was "Rainbow" Division. It reflected the composition of the division — representing all of America, made up of men selected from each state of the Union, stretching from one end of America to the other.

Recreating the last days of combat from my grandfather's point of view as a member of Company B, 142D Combat Engineer Battalion, presented some obvious problems for me. On the one hand, I wanted to write a book with a factual account that would stand on its own. On the other hand, I didn't want the book's narrative to get lost under a bunch of historical facts, details and such. I ended up sticking to facts, but I did so in as wide ranging a way as possible.

The end result is a book containing varying kinds of information. Anything in direct quotes was taken by interview, audiotape, in person or on the telephone. Dialogue based on the recollections of people, including me, appears in dialogue form as well. Quotes from published material have been condensed in some paragraphs to better fit the text. As previously noted, the audiotape of my grandfather, in his own words, is also in direct quotes, edited as little as possible for grammar and clarity.

I have written as complete an account as possible of my grandfather's experience in World War II. Unfortunately, there were some areas of his story that he was hesitant to fully elaborate on, such as what he experienced as he went through the horrific Dachau concentration camp. The passage of time also played a part. He passed away only six years after the audiotape was made. Everything he experienced is something that can never be fully known.

For me, researching my grandfather's account of the war led to a sobering conclusion: He did not expect to make it back from the war alive. He had accepted the grim reality that the odds of survival while in combat were not in his favor.

He mentioned that as he thought back to those times in battle, even though he didn't know it at the time, he was actually on the threshold of God's holy dwelling place — just one heartbeat away from stepping into eternity.

Though sure to be debated by some, the title, *Mount of Congregation*, is used as a reference to heaven, a holy realm above all. Even modern physics points to the reality of other dimensional existences.

I hope that in some way this book honors the service members and civilians who lost their lives in World War II, gives comfort to the families who still grieve for them, and serves as a reminder to future generations to never forget the sacrifices made on their behalf. Most of all, I hope this book demonstrates to the reader how God had a plan for my grandfather's life and was working behind the scenes to accomplish His will.

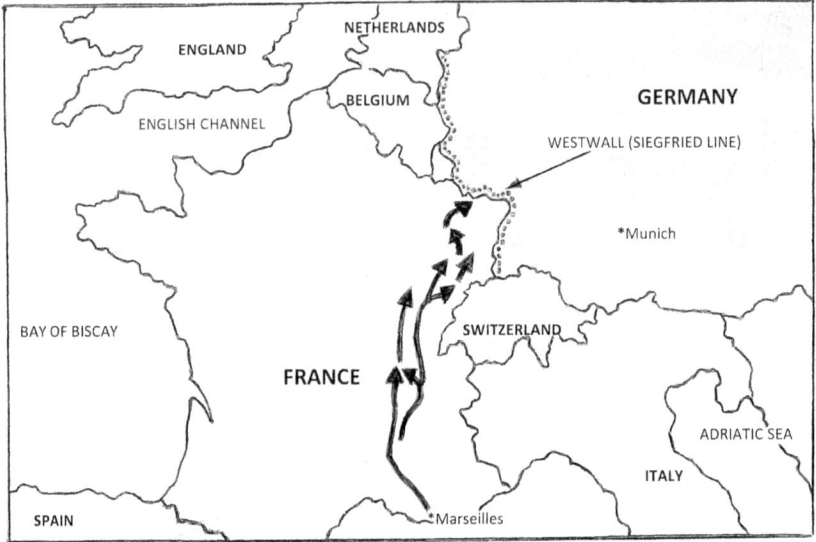

42nd Infantry "Rainbow" Division's thrust toward the Westwall.

TABLE OF CONTENTS

KELLY

It stalked into camp when the day was damp
And chilly and cold.
It crept by the guards
And murdered my pards
With a hand that was clammy and bony and bold;
And its breath was icy and moldy and dank,
And it killed so speedy
And gloatingly greedy
That it took away men from each company rank.
(From "The Flu" by Private Josh Lee, 1919)

My grandfather, Blace Edward Davis, was born in Grayson County, Virginia, on September 7, 1915. His parents were John Emmett Davis and Vera Virginia Shumate. There were no radios, no TV and no Internet back in those days. He was raised up in a Christian home and attended services at Mount Vale United Methodist Church. The family also included the recently widowed Betty Ellen Brown Davis, J.E.'s mother, who lived with them.

Times were tough for just about everyone living in the rural rugged Appalachian Mountains during that period. Transportation was still mostly on horseback and buggy. You could catch a train if you had the money — that is, if the local town you were near had a depot in the first place. Any sustained employment was hard to come by.

Blace's father, J.E. Davis, was determined to make something of himself, and started working in carpentry. It was rumored that he came to the mountains of Virginia with nothing more than a hammer and saw. Anything from a shed to a barn, if it needed to be built, his father was quick to offer his service.

In the early years, there were only a few jobs, but J.E. continued to excel in the trade of carpentry. This was mostly due to his strong work ethic. Each completed job only continued to build upon his reputation. In just a short while, he became known as an excellent carpenter. He was making a name for himself, and business was growing. His family was also growing when Virginia gave birth to another son, whom she named Kelly.

J.E.'s construction reputation eventually led to an opportunity for more promising work deep in the mountains of Pike County, Kentucky, on the border of West Virginia. This would require a move for his family. If only he knew what was about to happen in the next few years, he never would have made that move.

The family packed up and crossed the state line into Kentucky. Blace's brother Kelly was two years old upon their arrival into Pikes County and became the big brother of a newborn named Emmett in the fall of 1918. World War I was coming to an end overseas in Europe, but many Americans families would soon find themselves facing a war of their own.

During my training as a physician assistant, we studied historical cases involving pandemics — epidemics of infectious disease that spread through the human population and across continents. One such case we studied involved a virus known as the Spanish flu.

American troops returning from overseas brought back with them a deadly mutated virus. This particular strain of flu ravaged the Army camps across the nation. What started out with hundreds of victims eventually led to thousands who were felled by the often deadly disease.

On September 29, 1918, a U.S. Army physician at Fort Devens described the rapid clinical course of fatal influenza: "These men start with what appears to be an ordinary attack of La Grippe or Influenza, and when brought to the Hospital they very rapidly develop the most vicious type of Pneumonia that has ever been seen. Two hours after admission they have the Mahogany spots over the cheekbones, and a few hours later you can begin to see the cyanosis extending from their ears and spreading all over the face, until it is hard to distinguish the colored men from the white. It is only a matter of a few hours then until death comes, and it is simply a struggle for air until they suffocate. It is horrible." ("Camp Devens Letter," British Medical Journal, 22 December 1979; Vol 2, issue 1632.)

This strain of flu continued its devastating spread, even into the civilian population. One mysterious aspect of the pandemic was that those who were killed were mostly healthy young people, rather than the elderly and debilitated, as was the case with other diseases.

The spread of the flu virus was due to close contact with an infected individual, usually by way of a cough or sneeze. Described as the greatest medical holocaust in history, the pandemic killed millions worldwide. This was due to bacterial pneumonia — a common and deadly complication, as there were no antibiotics at that time to fight infections. Penicillin would not be discovered until 1928 by Scottish scientist Alexander Fleming.

The state of Kentucky was hit especially hard. Nearly every family lost someone. Gravediggers could not keep up with the demands for their services. For several weeks they maintained a backlog of graves that needed to be dug. Burials were quick and funerals banned, as were all other public meetings. Churches were closed, and local theaters were shut down.

There were severe shortages of doctors, nurses and medical supplies — and even caskets. Entire communities found themselves without any type of medical aid.

The pandemic left Kentucky and most of the United States as quickly and mysteriously as it had arrived. It was reported to have subsided in the state by the end of 1918. One can only imagine the fear that was present in the hearts of J.E. and his wife, Virginia, as they kept protective watch over their little ones during that time.

A new year had begun, and the Davis family was hesitantly starting to have a little hope in their surroundings. Just as they were beginning to think the worst was over, the flu hit the Davis household. J.E. and Virginia were soon bedridden due to the flu's devastating effects on their lungs. Blace's grandmother, Betty, had her hands full trying to take care of them. A few hours later, Kelly, my grandfather's two-year-old little brother, came down with a cough and fever. Within a few short days, he would succumb to the deadly virulent strain. Blace and Emmett would somehow miraculously survive the outbreak without even catching the flu.

Blace was just a little over four years old when Kelly died. They were inseparable as brothers. He remembered his grandmother having to arrange for Kelly's body to be removed from the house for burial, as his parents were still bedridden from the flu. The burial was quickly performed by local gravediggers, as funerals were still banned. His parents were inconsolable. Blace recalled holding his grandmother's hand while they watched from a distance as his brother was being buried. His grandmother placed a simple rock for a headstone, which was later inscribed with the initials "K.D."

In psychology, there is a term, "flashbulb memories." These are memories seared into the mind. Such was the case in the early months of 1919. The sadness of those moments were so strong that, in an instant, they were etched a little deeper than other memories in the mind of a four-year-old boy … forever. Blace would never forget his brother Kelly.

EYEWITNESS ACCOUNT

Behold, this stone shall be a witness unto us, for it hath heard all the words of the Lord which he spoke unto us: it shall be therefore a witness unto you.

(Joshua 24:27, King James Version)

I still have it: an audio cassette family interview dated May 8, 1985. It was made by one of my cousins as he recorded our grandfather at age 70. The family wanted to have our grandpa on tape, in his own words, as a firsthand account of what being in war was like. This was the same year that my grandfather's division, the Army's 42nd Infantry Division, was recognized as a liberating unit by the U.S. Army's Center of Military History and the United States Holocaust Memorial Museum.

World War II was the most widespread war in history. It was the biggest and most terrible war that has ever been fought. Millions upon millions of people were killed — half of them civilians, while the other half were soldiers, sailors and airmen. More than 400,000 of those who lost there lives were Americans. Even today, worldwide casualty estimates from several sources vary widely.

Yad Vashem: The World Holocaust Remembrance Center in Israel gives the following statistics regarding the number of

Jews killed in the Holocaust: "The figure commonly used is the six million, quoted by Adolf Eichmann, a senior SS official. All the serious research confirms that the number of victims was between five and six million."

As a kid in the late 1970s, years before the audio cassette tape recording was made, I can recall visiting my grandparent's home on many occasions with my family. My earliest memories were when they lived just across the practice field from Galax High School on Long Street. Our house was just a few miles away, so it was not unusual to frequently stop by and visit on our way to town. Grandpa had just gotten out of the hospital after having a heart attack and was beginning to slow down during this period of his life. Our parents would load me and my two brothers in the station wagon and make the short trip over to their home.

As soon as we arrived, my brothers and I were out of the car, chasing each other. Back then, kids our age played outside the majority of the time. It was the middle of autumn — the perfect time of the year to enjoy the cooler weather and the beautiful majestic surroundings of the Appalachian Mountains. The colorful leaves had already changed and were beginning to fall softly to the ground.

Our father bypassed the front door and went around to the back of the house. He had some work to do with raking the leaves and giving the yard a final mowing. My mother went inside to check and see if my grandparents needed anything. In later years, at my grandmother's funeral, my mom told that her mother-in-law had actually been her best friend.

My two brothers eventually chased me inside, through

the front door. We were immediately grabbed by my mom and scolded for running inside the house. Grandpa laughed as he saw us getting caught.

He was a builder by trade and one of the most humble men you could ever meet. His father had started a construction business shortly before World War II. My grandpa and two of his brothers, Jim and George, took over the business upon their father's death after the war. Their construction company, J.E. Davis & Sons, was known throughout southwest Virginia for constructing public schools, churches, banks and many other buildings, including the Smyth County Community Hospital in Marion and the Twin County Community Hospital in Galax, Virginia. They also constructed the student center building and the school of architecture building at Virginia Tech, Carroll County and Galax high schools, and Wytheville Community College, just to name a few. In the early 1950s, his brother George also helped in the construction of Philpott Dam in Henry and Franklin counties in Virginia, and later took over running the company.

I always looked forward to visiting with my grandpa. He was the one who gave me my first job. I was twelve years old. He had called over to our house and asked to speak with my dad. After a few short words, my father got off the phone, looked me straight in the eye, and told me to ride my bicycle to Grandpa's house. I didn't know what was going on, but I did what I was told.

My grandparents had recently moved to a house much closer to us. The house was built on a lot just across the street from Camp Zion Church, where Grandpa was pastor. He planned on having the house used as a parsonage. It took me just a few minutes to get there as I quickly pedaled up the road through our neighborhood. I hopped off my bicycle in the front yard and knocked on the door.

Grandma opened the door, gave me a big hug, and told me that Grandpa was waiting for me in the basement. I made my way past the kitchen and out to a side hallway where the stairs were located. It was a modest brick home with an unfinished basement. Part of the basement was roughly designed as a small wood shop for all kinds of projects. I can still remember the smell of the wood, sawdust on the floor, the various tools, as well as the warmth of the place. There was also the all-familiar flickering and snapping of a fire in the medium-sized black Mama Bear wood stove.

"Come here — I want to show you something," said Grandpa.

Parked just outside the basement was his old red Snapper lawnmower. I noticed he had a small trailer hitched to the rear with a load of dirt on it. He grinned, handed me the keys, told me to be careful and drive the lawnmower from his house over to Mr. Higgins, who lived about a mile from him on Cardinal Road.

I thought he was kidding. At twelve years of age, some people might call this dangerous. I suppose in Grandpa's eyes, twelve was old enough to start taking on some responsibility. I had been on this lawnmower before when my dad would mow the lawn. He would sometimes let me operate the mower as he watched protectively just a few yards away. This time was different. It would be the first time I would be on my own — at least that was the impression in my small mind.

My feet barely touched the clutch as I awkwardly left Grandpa's yard, towing the trailer of dirt as I looked both ways before entering the road. I changed from first to third gear and was well on my way. What I didn't know was that Grandpa had already called ahead and Mr. Higgins was expecting me in just a few minutes. There were also several neighbors he had contacted as well, who would be watching as I passed by their homes. I guess you could say the eyes of our neighborhood were upon me as I made my way hauling my little cargo of dirt. I could not understand why he picked me to do the job, but I know it made me feel like a real man on my way back to his house when the task was completed.

Family was a big deal to my grandparents. They always had my aunts and uncles stay with them when they came in for visits. One particular time, when my cousins were in for a family gathering, Grandpa took me and my two brothers, along with my two cousins, down to his wood shop in the basement. Our ages ranged from around eleven to thirteen years old at the time.

We all gathered around the Mama Bear stove. Next to the stove was a section of the basement where he had an old metallic gray wall locker. We found that this was a good spot to hang out. On cold mornings, the warmth from the wood stove would actually bounce off the wall locker, making a comfortable place to enjoy the heat. At times he would have us in the basement helping him tinker with some woodworking projects. Thinking back now, I assume it was just a way for him to spend some quality time with his grandchildren.

We were becoming teenagers, and my older brother had enough courage to ask him if he would tell us about the war. We knew from our parents that he had been in World War II. He never talked much about what he saw but at times did share a little of his experiences with the congregation at his church. Some of what he was about to tell us would later be captured on audiotape.

When the question was asked, he paused for a moment, as if he was searching for a reason not to tell us about the war. Looking back now, I guess I could see in his eyes that he wanted to keep his grandchildren from some of the terrible realities of this world. But I also assume he realized the five grandchildren standing around him were getting older. In a few short years, we would also be adults.

He turned and reached into his pocket. He pulled out a key and unlocked the wall locker. In the bottom of the locker was a small box. I still remember the first time he shared with us what was inside.

After opening the box, he pulled out a dust-covered blue book and laid it on his carpenter's work table. It had the words "42nd 'Rainbow' Infantry Division" on the front cover. There were also pictures, a few ribbons and medals, a Purple Heart, German postcards, a Hitler Youth knife, and even some coins. One coin was about the size of a penny and had the Third Reich symbol stamped onto it. There was also his division insignia patch, which resembled a rainbow in bright red, gold and blue colors.

My grandfather was attached to Company B 142D Engineer Combat Battalion for the 42nd Infantry Rainbow Division. This battalion-strength combat engineering unit was one of several such battalions that participated in the final Allied invasion into Germany. Combat engineers are a component of the U.S. Army Corps of Engineers. They were best known for pontoon bridge construction. Each man was trained in hand-to-hand combat, the use of defensive machine guns, grenade launchers and anti-tank rockets, and required to fight as infantry when called upon. Experts in the deployment and deactivation of explosive charges and unexploded munitions, they were also skilled in camouflage and a wide variety of construction services that proved crucial in support of frontline troops. Combat engineers played a crucial role in the final Allied offensive attack into Germany.

The insignia patch and other items were passed around so that each of us could hold them in our hands. We were amazed at what he was showing us. He sat down beside his work bench and opened the book. We huddled in close as he began to read some sections from it. His reading was at times interrupted with more questions from us, but that did not seem to bother him. He could tell he had our attention, and he appeared to become more comfortable with what he was about to share. Grandpa then began to tell us his story. I still remember his words.

"It took us twelve days to go over," he said.

A Sense of Urgency

"Think instead of the possibility, however remote it may be, that we may be needed on an active front in a very short time. Prepare yourselves for the possibility, and be serious in your preparations."

(Major General Harry J. Collins Division Commander, 42nd Infantry Rainbow Division)

Twelve days. That was the time it took for the soldiers to get from Camp Kilmer, New Jersey, to Marseille, France. It was January 1945. In Germany, war had been raging, and the Battle of the Bulge was still ongoing.

Just a few short months after being drafted, the men of Company B 142D Engineer Combat Battalion were getting to the end of their intensive training at Camp Gruber, Oklahoma. Word came from Command that more soldiers were needed in Europe immediately because of what was happening in Germany. This also affected the length of time available for training. Now it would be condensed, as the men focused not only on the engineer side of their training but also on the essentials of combat. My grandfather's battalion was quickly given the assignment to move out. Hundreds of soldiers loaded onto the long trains made up of Pullman coaches and troop sleepers. Locals waved flags and cheered, but some were crying as the trains slowly made their way out. They knew a lot of the boys would not be returning home. The trip from Oklahoma to New Jersey would take more than two days.

Upon arrival at Camp Kilmer, final preparations for the long ocean voyage to Marseille, France, were being made. In-processing, equipment checks, medical — more vaccinations — and clothing checks were being carried out. A few days later, taking advantage of a twelve-hour pass in New York City, many chose to see the sights off base, while others stayed behind and contemplated what lay ahead overseas. Hundreds wrote final letters home to loved ones. A few even took the opportunity to call home one last time after standing in line for hours at telephone centers.

Command sent word for all soldiers outside of base to return to Camp Kilmer. Orders were given to join up with the three other infantry regiments known as Task Force Linden, which had previously rushed in ahead of the division overseas at the end of fall 1944. The gates of Camp Kilmer were soon locked down, and phone calls were restricted. On January 6, 1945, the men of Company B 142D Engineer Combat Battalion boarded troop ships destined for France. In a matter of weeks, they would be heading directly into Germany's active front in the shortest amount of time possible.

"It was a sight to see," Grandpa said. "Ships from our convoy covered one horizon to the other as we left the mainland."

Prior to my grandfather's arrival in Germany, the men of Task Force Linden found themselves fragmented, trying desperately to prevent Hitler's German army from breaking out in Alsace, a region in eastern France on the west bank of the upper Rhine adjacent to Germany and Switzerland. It was the dead of winter. The Americans were stretched thin, fragmented, with little to no backup or support. The weather was cold, and frost bite was all too common. One infantryman was reported to have stated they were "flung into the maw" as they tried to hold their positions, defending as they attacked and counterattacked the powerful German forces.

The Battle of the Bulge was the largest battle fought on the Western Front in Europe during World War II — and also the largest battle ever fought by the United States Army. My grandfather said this surprise attack by the Germans, who thrust their forces into the Allied front lines, was the main reason they were being sent overseas into Europe. The battle began on December 16, 1944, just a few weeks prior to my grandfather's arrival into Europe. It was so named because of the some sixty-mile "bulge" the Germans' blitzkrieg left in the Allied lines. It was an audacious counterattack against the U.S. and Allied forces by the Germans, which began in the freezing Ardennes Forest in southern Belgium and Luxembourg.

In the Taunus Mountains of Germany lay Kransberg Castle. Underneath the castle was the fortified Adlerhorst bunker, where Adolf Hitler was planning his next move against the Allies. Three days prior to launching an offensive move against the Allies known as "Operation Nordwind," he had declared in a speech to division commanders on December 28, 1944: "This attack has a very clear objective, namely the destruction of the enemy forces. There is not a matter of prestige involved here. It is a matter of destroying and exterminating the enemy forces wherever we find them." This last major offensive by the powerful German forces would begin on December 31, 1944, in Alsace.

By January 15, 1945, the U.S. VI Corps found themselves having to fight on three sides, bearing the brunt of the German attacks. Army casualties were high, and the men were running short on reinforcements, as well as ammunition, tanks and supplies. Supreme Allied Commander, U.S. Gen. Eisenhower, hurriedly moved his battered divisions from the Ardennes southeast across more than sixty miles to reinforce the 7th Army. The move, however, was delayed, and the American forces were forced to withdraw to defensive positions. The German offensive finally drew to a close on January 25, 1945. This was due to the U.S. 222nd Infantry Regiment stopping their advance near Haguenau, where they repulsed repeated attacks by the German 7th Parachute and 47th VG Divisions. They would earn the Presidential Unit Citation in the process. This was the same day that the reinforcements began to arrive from the Ardennes Forest.

Passing through the Strait of Gibraltar, with Africa on one side and Europe on the other, my grandfather's convoy of ships headed toward the Mediterranean port of Marseille, France. Evidently they had encountered some rough seas on the way over.

He recalled that at first they had good weather as the troop ships left the U.S. mainland. A few days later, the weather worsened as the troop ships plunged headlong through the stormy waters toward Marseille. (I can still remember him preaching in church, describing what it was like to be in a storm at sea. One Sunday, in the middle of his sermon, he recalled being down below in the tight berthing quarters on board the troop ship. "The men were packed in like sardines," he said. "You literally had to crawl over the soldiers beside you to get from one section of the ship to the next.")

As the weather continued to worsen, the men did whatever they could to take their minds off the relentless, sickening motion of the sea. "Some were playing cards, others were telling stories. A few were sick," he said.

My grandfather, Blace, had enough of these cramped quarters after ten days. He decided to go up top for a quick view of what was happening outside. Because of the danger of German U-boats, there were strict orders for no lights outside at night, as even the flicker of a cigarette could compromise the ship's location in wartime. He was outside for only a second when the ship suddenly lunged and struck a wave with such force that it felt as if it might break in half. The crashing waves covered the deck of the ship. He quickly returned below and later recalled that the waves looked larger than mountains on both sides of the vessel.

Over the next two days, the sea improved enough to make landfall. The convoy arrived in the port of Marseille on January 18, 1945. The men of Company B were thankful to have their feet on solid ground after the twelve-day voyage. Orders were given for each soldier to take his military gear and prepare to exit the ship. They quickly formed lines and headed to the gangway. Grandpa recalled that as they left the vessel their exposed faces were immediately greeted by an icy cold north wind.

"That wind carried a strange sense of urgency," he said.

The soldiers began the arduous task of moving their

equipment inland through the snow-covered ground. Company B was ordered to take its men to a staging area on top of a hill above Marseille. It was about ten miles away from the city, a large, barren piece of land with no trees, and exposed to the wintry weather. Blace could see a few lights of the city in the distance as night began to fall. This parcel of ground was known as Command Post 2.

"We nicknamed the place 'Pneumonia Knob,'" he said. He recalled some of the men became sick after having to make camp on the stone-cold, windswept piece of ground. It was freezing. But having to sleep outdoors with nothing but a sleeping bag and tent was only a foretaste of what lay ahead.

Within a few days of arriving at Command Post 2, the soldiers were about to hear what the first part of their mission would entail. Officers instructed the men to come in close as a few plans were revealed and orders given.

"All we were told was that we would soon go into combat somewhere, but where was not revealed," Grandpa said.

What he didn't know at the time was that they were to join up with the rest of the Allied forces by advancing north from the port of Marseille up the Rhone River Valley, and then head northeast toward the Siegfried Line in Germany. They would relieve the 45th Infantry Division on the front lines between France and Germany in an area near Wimmenau and Wingen, in the Hardt Mountains northwest of Haguenau, France. The men and equipment would travel by slow-moving troop trains heading north for part of the way, then by truck convoy — along with days of seemingly never-ending marching — through the wintry landscape. It would take the men and equipment approximately three weeks to get there.

The Siegfried Line stretched from the northwestern town of Kleve on the border with the Netherlands, along the western border of Germany, as far south as the town of Weil am Rhein on the border of Switzerland. This defensive line for Germany was actually a series of thousands of fortified bunkers, machine gun nests, tank traps and pillboxes with concrete, dug-in guard posts, normally equipped with loopholes through which the Germans fired their weapons. It was all planned in 1936 by Hitler and built between 1938 and 1940.

Grandpa told us that after the war it was said that the Siegfried Line Campaign was similar to the Battle of Normandy. Instead of hedgerows, the Allies encountered deadly pillboxes, densely wooded forests, canals, booby traps, and urban snares. These obstacles made it quite difficult for the American soldier to go very far, very fast, under those conditions, until overwhelming tactical and logistical strength could be built up.

From September 1944 to March 1945, this defensive line was subject to a large-scale Allied offensive. The overall cost of this campaign was close to 140,000 American lives.

Some of this was due to the large number of deadly pillboxes and machine gun nests. In an intelligence bulletin article entitled "Pillbox Warfare in the Siegfried Line," dated January 1945, rifle company commanders gave insight into German pillbox warfare. This intelligence was then used to assist American soldiers in getting ready for the upcoming Allied invasion through the Siegfried Line and into Germany. The information was shared with many of the men, including my grandfather, who were about to take part in the upcoming assault.

Commanders of four U.S. rifle companies noted to have been in contact with the enemy provided intelligence of great worth concerning the resistance offered by the deadly pillboxes located along the Siegfried Line. This information primarily focused on the vulnerability of those fortifications but warned the soldiers of their deadly capabilities as well.

The bulletin discussed three types of pillboxes: some had one slit opening through which to shoot; others employed mounted machine guns and and had two slit openings; while other pillboxes were used simply as enemy personnel shelters. The pillboxes were located approximately 100 yards apart and mutually supportive against an attacking force.

Most of the surrounding terrain presented obstacles for the Allies' tanks, with steep hills (some as high as 500 feet), thick forests, underbrush, creeks, and streams. The majority of the pillboxes and machine-gun nests were camouflaged by the surrounding terrain.

The intelligence bulletin strongly advised the U.S. soldier who was about to be a part of the assault force into Germany not only to know his weapon and job responsibility, but also to know the weapon and job responsibility of the soldier beside him.

The bulletin described what the soldiers would likely encounter when battling a German pillbox. Such an assault would typically begin with a barrage of forward automatic weapon fire by U.S soldiers, hopefully causing the pillbox to close up. However, the bulletin warned the soldiers that even when pillboxes were closed or buttoned up, the Germans could still fire through the small forward slits with deadly accuracy. The goal of the assault was to get men to the blind side of the pillbox and engage with TNT explosives, including a pole charge against the door.

The bulletin went on to warn against letting anybody approach the rear area of the pillbox. The Germans were known to keep this area covered by way of a small opening, a slit, through which deadly machine gun fire could be poured onto an advancing force.

At no time was any U.S. soldier allowed to enter a pillbox in order to take prisoners. The bulletin advised making prisoners exit the pillbox. The commanders of the rifle company who wrote the bulletin also noted that if the enemy claimed to be injured and would not come out, a second charge of TNT would somehow encourage them to comply.

Other assault methods were covered, including the use of tank-dozers. These specially designed tanks could be used on the fortifications located at lower levels, pushing dirt forward, essentially burying the pillbox and entombing the enemy combatants. Tank blasts to the rear of the pillbox could also be used to destroy the fortifications — depending on whether the tank could get into position in the first place, given the mountainous terrain expected to be encountered.

The intelligence also advised that once a fortification was taken, it must be destroyed completely — leveled to the ground. If even one wall was left standing, the enemy could regroup and use what was left of the structure as a location from which to fight. In some instances, pillboxes had to be retaken on multiple occasions because the fortifications were not completely destroyed the first time.

In only a matter of weeks, the men of Company B would encounter this deadly maze of pillbox fortifications. They would soon be taking part in the final Allied invasion, entering first through the Siegfried Line, and then into the heart of Nazi Germany, also known as the Third Reich, controlled by the *führer* himself. It was at this time that, spontaneously and without direct orders, each man befriended another fellow soldier who became his "battle buddy." This was known to have occurred to troops about to enter combat. They would share foxholes together, mess together, comfort each other, and fight together.

CONSCRIPTION

"So they gave you a choice?" asked my cousin. "No," he said, "they acted like they were going to give me a choice. I said I'd like to be a Marine. The officer looked at the other officer and said, 'Put him in the Army — they need him.'"

(Audiocassette interview, May 8, 1985)

Springtime had come early to Jacksonville, North Carolina. Blace was a young married man with a growing family — six children and one on the way. He had likely not given much thought to the possibility of being drafted into the war. A few years prior, in 1941, he was initially labeled by the draft board as Class 3-A — man with dependents. The likelihood of him being drafted was next to zero.

He was at a point in his life where he wanted to strike out on his own, away from his father's construction business in Virginia. He respected his father's achievement and competence. As the eldest son, he had seen his father build a business from nothing, which was no mean task. He decided to apprise his father of the realities: that he needed an area of freedom and an independent way to develop more skills and responsibilities. He was given a choice: He could do so within the company's framework or, if not feasible, outside it. He chose the latter.

He landed a promising job as a carpenter on a defense project at Marine Corps Base Camp Lejeune and moved his family to North Carolina. The work was plentiful and the pay was good. The project was also using some of the best skilled workers in the construction business.

Blace's oldest son, Richard (my uncle), later recalled in a letter to one of his sisters what it was like during that time.

It was exciting to us children being in a new and strange place. We did cry and whine a lot about the drinking water that smelled and tasted like sulphur and longed for a drink from the cold spring at Poplar Grove, but seeing the ocean for the first time was exciting. We were allowed only to wade, since none of the family had bathing suits. One day Dad took us fishing in a row boat in Pamlico Sound. We used drop cords and would catch spot and croaker two at a time. I hooked a sand shark that splashed all of us in the boat before getting away. Dad broke a paddle, and we were towed in by a passing boat, which was a good thing since the tide was taking us farther out to sea.

From time to time we would have "blackouts" on the coast. All cars were required to have the top half of their lights painted black. Gasoline and other things were rationed. Sometimes people would try mixing kerosene with gasoline, hoping to get a few extra miles of travel from their rationed amount.

Dad and I went duck hunting on the New River in Jacksonville on Thanksgiving Day in 1943. We borrowed a boat, and he paddled us up and down the river looking for ducks. I don't recall seeing any ducks, but I do recall it being a very desolate wooded area. As we were leaving, our car sank into the soft sand and became stuck halfway through an open gate. We could not leave the area unattended because livestock would get out. Dad gave me a choice of staying there alone or going for help through the woods. By this time, it was dark, and I could not stand the thought of staying there alone. Adrenaline flowing and heart pounding, I ran as fast as I could through the wooded portion, jumping mud holes in the unpaved road and not stopping until reaching the lights of the neighborhood. I led Mom, a neighbor, and the rest of the family back to dad. We easily pushed the car out of the sand and through the gate.

I recall the family going into Jacksonville to check our mail at the post office. Dad returned to the car with his "call." It was a shock to all of us. I remember it being a quiet and somber time for the family, which was unusual in those days. We packed our few things and left for Galax, Virginia, almost immediately.

My grandfather was twenty-eight years old and the father of six children when he got drafted. He described that moment as his "calling" from the president of the United States. He was now listed as class 1-A: available for military service.

"How could a father with that many children be sent off to war?" asked my dad.

That was a question that lingered for years after the war, and yet my dad never seemed to get a satisfying answer. He was what my grandmother called a "war baby." His mother, Alma, was just a few months pregnant when her husband was drafted.

In the early days of the draft, men with dependents were deferred from having to enlist. The draft boards were made up of local men. These men were also given a quota of draftees, and the quota had to be met. Each draft board began by drafting all the 1-A men, men who were available for military service. Once the 1-A candidates were depleted, they drafted men with limited deferments until they reached their quota. Since the draft board members were all local, they were presumed to know a little about the men they were drafting.

As the war progressed, more and more men were needed for the armed forces. By 1944, there was a huge manpower shortage. Married men with children classified as 3-A were initially deferred, but now they were being re-classified as 1-A by the draft boards. Having dependents was no longer a reason to keep men from being drafted into the war effort.

When Blace received that draft letter, it changed his plans drastically. He could not believe he was actually being drafted, yet he would not dispute the reclassification. Alma pleaded with him to find some way not to go. There was nothing medically wrong with him. There were certainly draft dodgers during that time, but he would have no part in that. He needed to make some plans, and he needed to make them quickly. He still had a small house back in Virginia. There was also family back home who could help with the children. His wife's mother and father lived just a few houses down from them.

When he was drafted in the spring of 1944, Blace was ordered to return to his home state for his armed forces physical examination. Soon his car was packed and on the road with his family. It was an unusually quiet and somber moment as the family began their journey back through the foothills and into Virginia. Along the way, there was a feeling of uncertainty about what the future held.

Day after day, he had seen the Marines training at Camp Lejeune, and he respected what he saw. If he had a say in what branch of service he would be called into, he would become a "leatherneck" — a Marine. This would never happen. The letter he had received from the local draft board with an "order to report for induction" named the Army as the branch of service he was being called to. It included the date, time, and place where the paperwork would be filled out and an examination given. He was also informed to get his affairs in order and say his last goodbyes.

Unbeknownst to Blace, Alma tried one last time to find some reason the father of her children would not have to go to war — by approaching and literally begging the hometown doctor to find him unfit. She was told by the doctor there was nothing he could do.

My grandfather's hope of becoming a Marine was denied when he appeared at Roanoke, Virginia, for examination. He was later officially inducted into the Army at Fort George G. Meade, Maryland, on April 1, 1944. His country needed him as a combat engineer in the United States Army.

By the summer of 1944, he was finishing up with his basic training at the Infantry Replacement Training Center located in Fort McClellan, Alabama. Nearly 500,000 men were trained at Fort McClellan during World War II. It was here where recruits were taught their basic soldiering skills.

One of my cousins asked Grandpa the following question about how he arrived for basic training.

"Did they fly you out there, or did you get on a bus?"

"I flew on a train," he responded.

CORDUROY ROADS

Contend, O Lord, with those who contend with me; Fight against those who fight against me.

(Psalm 35:1, King James Version)

On September 23, 1944, Blace arrived at Camp Gruber, Oklahoma, for more intensive training as a combat engineer. The training also included ongoing preparations for overseas duty.

It was here that he would be introduced to another type of weapon. Blace was already familiar with his standard issue rifle: the M-1 carbine, a lightweight, easy-to-use, .30 caliber semi-automatic rifle. He was now training with a heavy machine gun: the M-2 Browning.

Referred to as the "Ma Deuce," The M-2 was an effective .50 caliber machine gun against infantry, light-armored vehicles and boats, light fortifications and low-flying aircraft. More and more soldiers in Company B were being trained in its use. Grandpa noted that this was likely in response to intelligence reports of the Germans' widespread use of automatic weapons.

"These types of weapons were already making a difference in the war," he said. "They were expected to see even more use during the planned upcoming final Allied advance into Germany."

"Did you ever have to shoot someone?" I asked.

Grandpa suddenly got up from where he was sitting beside his work bench and placed another log in the wood stove. You could hear a pin drop as my brothers and cousins waited on his answer. I am sure they too wanted to know his response, as any kid would. He turned from the stove while giving me a stern look.

"I never had to shoot at anybody up close," he responded.

We never asked him that question again.

I thought such a question might end the story, but he returned to his seat and then pulled out one of the coins from the box and held it up close to our faces. It was a Hitler's Third Reich coin, with a swastika stamped onto it. He continued with his story.

Following the advancing infantry along with the rest of the engineer battalion, the men of Company B made their way up north through the snow-covered Rhone River Valley of France. Earlier in the week, it had snowed more than a foot. They were well over a week into their mission and were beginning to make a turn for the northeast.

His objective as a combat engineer was to repair the roads and get the roads ready for the men and equipment as they inched their way through the rugged wintry terrain, heading toward the front line. This was a dangerous part of the mission, as they were also encountering German forces along the way.

These areas were some of the most rugged they had encountered. The region was heavily wooded, with steep mountains. This was extremely difficult terrain, especially for the soldiers on foot who were loaded down with battle gear and weapons.

Off in the distance, Blace heard his first explosion and an exchange of gunfire. The sporadic gunfire echoed down through the valley before fading away. This caused the men to pause for a moment before continuing forward.

Moving heavy equipment like tanks, jeeps, and trucks was nearly impossible. At one point, the men were bogged down due to the mud and melting snow. Several jeeps and trucks were stuck in the mess. They were ordered to keep moving forward. But how?

"It was muddy, real muddy," said Grandpa. "I remember when I was in the third grade, one of the readers told about the old corduroy roads that they used to have back in the pioneer days. They would cut trees down and lay them crossways — cross the road and put them right together — that would keep them from bogging down.

"We cut down a bunch of trees and put them side by side — maybe about a hundred foot long — then we had a good time standing on one side laughing at the officers going through there on their jeeps. They were bouncing up and down ... we couldn't hardly hold our mirth. We were really having a time at that. Finally, there was a jeep that took the smiles off of our faces. The jeep went over and ... we noticed it. It was jarring, too, but we noticed something on the back of it: It was two dead soldiers. They were in their mattress cover."

Grandpa said that during the war each soldier was issued what looked like a "white mattress cover." He also recalled that they thought it was used just for sleeping, but, in actuality, it was used "for your shroud when they put you in ... you know ... when you got killed." This was the first time he had seen dead soldiers.

Grandpa stood up from where he was sitting as he cleared his throat. "We could see the blood on ... in places like that. It hurt us worse when we found out who they were. There was a captain that once went with us, and a lieutenant. They went out on a detail, and one of them stepped on a landmine. They called it a "Bouncing Betty." It looked like a blade of grass. You stepped on it, it would shoot up about this high and it would blow up. This captain stepped on the landmine, and it blew up and killed him. The lieutenant started running out to him, hollering 'Captain, Captain!' A machine gun got him … killed him. That took the fun out of watching them go across the rough place there."

The men continued pushing and pulling their equipment through the snow-covered mud, which was ankle-deep in some places, as they continued northeast. The further they went, the worse the roads became. This was due not only to the wintry weather; it was also because of congestion on the roads. As they headed toward the front, hundreds of civilians in long lines were fleeing in the opposite direction. A lucky few had mule-drawn wagon carts, but the majority were struggling with dog carts or pushing covered baby wagons loaded down with what few valuable possessions they could carry. The wagons and carts were also being pulled and pushed through the snow and mud by young and old alike. Some had even harnessed their dogs to the front of the wagons to help with the loads.

And then there were the children.

As Blace passed by the civilians, he made eye contact with a small child sitting on top of one of the carts. The child was covered with snow, shivering, and bundled up with what little clothing her family had to protect her from the elements. He could not help but think about his children back home in Virginia.

He remembered a moment shortly before leaving the States as his children wailed and cried, holding onto him and pleading with him not to leave. One of his brothers was there and could not tolerate what he was witnessing. His brother left the house and went over to their neighbor's house. His brother told their neighbor, "It's more than I can take — worse than a funeral." Those memories continued to play over and over in Blace's mind as he continued forward along the crowded roadway.

Not much was said as the men of Company B, bound for the outskirts of Wimmenau, passed by the civilians on that snow-covered road. They tried as best they could to help the civilians who struggled with their loads, but orders were given to keep moving. They were needed at the front. Off in the distance, faint gunfire could be heard periodically through the frigid wintry air. The soldiers continued forward. In just a few more days they would be at the front line.

OPERATION GREIF

"I want you to create special units wearing American and British uniforms. Think of the confusion you could cause!"

(Adolph Hitler)

By February 1945, as they approached the outer boundaries of the Siegfried Line to relieve the 45th Infantry Division, the men of Company B were learning that things were not what they appeared to be.

"What you thought you were looking at was not necessarily what you were actually seeing," Grandpa said.

He recalled being positioned with his battle buddy outside the entrance to a house which had all its windows blown out. They were just about a mile from the Germans' front line. The men entered the house to clear it and saw a photo of Hitler hanging on the front living room wall. He and his buddy were about to knock the picture off the wall with the butts of their rifles when they were abruptly stopped by a member of the 45th Infantry Division. This man's battle experience over the past month, fighting against Hitler's powerful German forces in the Battle of the Bulge, had saved their lives. The picture was attached to a trip wire and explosives. Such a device was intended to kill if triggered by the actions of its unknowing victims.

As they left the house, he noticed a small coin lying in one of his boot tracks on the snow-dusted ground. He reached down, picked up the coin and put it in his pocket. This was the same coin Grandpa was showing us as he continued with his story.

The men of the 45th Infantry Division, known as the "Thunderbirds," proved invaluable with such recent battle experience. One month prior to Blace's arrival in Europe, they were the first U.S. troops of the 7th Army to cross into the German homeland in December 1944. But, at almost the same time, on December 16, 1944, the Battle of the Bulge began northward in the Ardennes Forest. Because of this, Command gave orders to cease their offensive operation, withdraw to more defensive operations just inside of France and spread out to cover more territory. Such repositioning of U.S. divisions led to the 7th Army going on the defensive until the "bulge" could be reduced. From January 21 until March 13, 1945, they occupied defensive positions while the unit was rebuilt and trained for the upcoming attack designed to break through the Siegfried Line once and for all.

On February 14, Blace and the men arrived just behind the front lines to relieve the 45th Infantry Division in an area near Wimmenau and Wingen, in the Hardt Mountains northwest of Haguenau. Three days later, on February 17, the command of the sector was passed to Major General Harry J. Collins. The 42nd Infantry Division as a whole, which included the men of Company B 142D Engineer Combat Battalion, had now entered combat. Known as the Rainbow Division, they took up defensive positions near Haguenau, in the Hardt Forest. Little did they know that this was the first day of 114 days to come, all of which would be in direct combat with the enemy.

One of the first objectives for Rainbow Division was to aggressively step up the number of patrols and raids along the front line. This was done in order to determine the enemy's strengths and weaknesses prior to the planned final invasion into Germany.

Rainbow Division would initially be fighting against the German 6th Mountain Division, an experienced unit known for having trained in this same thick wooded area, which stretched for miles in front of them.

Hitler was doing all he could to create havoc behind the Allied lines. Since the beginning of the Battle of the Bulge, he had continued to assemble what some would call an "army of imposters." Under the command of Austrian SS commando Otto Skorzeny, the imposters were directed by Hitler to prepare for a top-secret mission known as "Operation *Greif*." Skorzeny would outfit English-speaking German soldiers with captured American uniforms, weapons, and even jeeps. These German soldiers would then slip behind the Allied lines and pose as U.S. soldiers. Their mission was to create confusion by cutting communication lines, switching road signs, and other acts of sabotage. When word came to the U.S. soldiers that German commandos were masquerading as Americans, the soldiers set up checkpoints and began grilling each passerby on passwords, American pop culture, and even baseball in order to confirm their identities.

Grandpa described one such episode:

"While we were working there one time, I was off to one side. The others were maybe fifty yards from me. A jeep came up. It just came running real fast up the road, this little old jeep trail in the woods there, and an officer got out.

"He looked like a movie star — fancy little mustache, you know — and he spoke fluent English. Real good English … too fluent! And his driver got out and put one foot up on the fender and held a submachine gun on me. And that fellow soldier said, 'What are you doing here?'

"I said, 'I tell you, Major — he had a major's insignia on — you had better go to the sergeant. He can tell you more about it than I can.' So the fellow stood right there and watched me just like I was an outlaw or something and held that gun right on me. The major turned around, just came quick step and jumped in the jeep and said, 'Let's go.' They rode off.

"My sergeant came out there and said, 'What do you think about that guy?' And I said, 'I don't know, he looked suspicious to me.' He said, 'Why didn't you spring the password on him?' I felt like saying why didn't he spring the password on him, but I didn't tell the sergeant that. Bound to have been a German officer, coming up there spying us out because we were getting ready to make the big push."

Hitler most likely had hoped that these types of incidents would cause confusion and suspicion for the U.S. soldiers on the front line. The wait for the final word to begin the invasion into Germany became even more nerve-wracking as the days progressed and the patrols continued.

One of the greatest fears my grandfather expressed was that he was always afraid he would run up on a German Nazi and wouldn't be able to get his weapon in shooting position fast enough. This fear was likely shared among many in their battalion as they awaited their orders to begin the invasion. The men of Company B 142D Engineer Combat Battalion had positioned themselves just behind the front infantry lines. Most of the men, including my grandfather, carried a loaded round in the chamber of their weapon.

One evening he was heading into camp to clean his weapon: "I went into camp and was cleaning my gun, thought I'd clean it before supper time," he told us. "The fellows were all getting ready to go to chow and I was trying to hurry. I wanted a clip in my gun.

"They are a little tricky. I put a clip up in there, and then I didn't want to leave pressure on my trigger spring because, having Army training, I knew it was important that you keep your pressure off your trigger spring. So I just pulled the lever back on my bolt, and I held my thumb down to keep the bullet from going in the chamber. So after I got the bolt back in place I held the gun straight up and pulled the trigger and KERAAAM!

"Boy, it exploded. And here comes the captain and first lieutenant. The first lieutenant said, 'Davis, where did that shot come from?' I dropped my head and said, 'Out of my gun, sir.' You talk about a chewing — they really chewed me. The first lieutenant said, 'The very idea of a soldier accidentally letting a gun go off right here in the middle of camp!' And I said, 'It wasn't accidentally, sir. I raised the barrel on it and pulled the trigger and there happened to be a load in it.' And he chewed me a little more."

We laughed as he told us that part of the story, but Grandpa did not. He reminded us that many of the men were just like him, exhausted and on edge.

He recalled that from the time they had arrived at the front, from Feb 14, 1945, until the middle of March 1945, the Army had continued to make thrusts toward the Germans' front line of defense. This would eventually reveal the enemy's strong points and weaknesses. These patrols and raids would prove crucial in determining where the final advance into Germany would take place.

On March 13, Rainbow Division received orders that the 7th Army, whom they were a part of, would advance as a whole on March 15 toward, and eventually into, Germany's Westwall, a network of defensive structures also known as the Siegfried Line. This ongoing offensive attack into Germany, once started, would last for months. It would not stop until the division reached the border of Austria.

The invasion was now imminent. The time and date had been chosen. "H-Hour" a term used by the U.S. military to describe the beginning of battle, was set to begin on March 15 for this major event. There would be no turning back for the men of Rainbow Division.

Grandpa looked up from where he was sitting and, point blank, asked us a question.

"How would you feel if you were put into the shoes of an infantry soldier at that time and hour?"

That was a good way of relating to us what was going on in his mind at that time. How would we respond knowing we were about to go into battle? Would we be brave enough? Would we fear for our lives? Would we take time to write that final letter home? Would we make it back? Those were some of the questions most of us were asking ourselves as we sat listening, huddled near the warmth of the Mama Bear stove. We were hanging onto every word as Grandpa continued.

"We moved on up to the front, and they told us we're going to hit the enemy today and we're not going to stop. We're not going to stop until we cross the Rhine River. And some of us went out and had a little prayer."

He told us the Germans had prepared defenses in the Hardt Mountains. This was soon to be the first area over which they were ordered to advance. It would also be remembered as some of the most rugged terrain they would ever encounter. The mountains were high and heavily wooded. The weather was improving somewhat. Even though it was getting a little warmer, there was still plenty of rain and mud to deal with.

At 0645 on the morning of March 15, 1945, after a month of extensive patrolling and active defense, 42nd Infantry Rainbow Division began their attack and went on the offensive. They would continue their advancement into Germany until they reached the border of Austria. For these men, this date would go down in history as the beginning of the final Allied advance into Germany.

THE IDES OF MARCH

On his way to the Theatre of Pompey, where he would be assassinated, Caesar passed the seer and joked, "The Ides of March are come," implying that the prophecy had not been fulfilled, to which the seer replied, "Aye, Caesar; but not gone."

(*Plutarch,* Parallel Lives*)*

Grandpa continued: "I had the best Christianity at one time. The boys depended a whole lot on my knowing a little something about the Bible. We went out and had our prayer meeting, and the next morning, bright and early, it was the 15th of March."

H-Hour had come for the entire 7th Army, which included the men of Rainbow Division. Their orders were to attack and make it to — and through — the Westwall.

There was an eerie silence in the initial hours of dawn as the assault by 42nd Rainbow Division began. This was a pre-planned attack, one in which a different tactic was imposed: The men moved out without prior artillery preparation. This took the Germans by complete surprise. The men continued to move forward into the prepared defenses of the Hardt Mountains with no initial opposition.

Suddenly the unnerving silence was broken by a rumbling

sound in the distance. German 88mm guns, among the most feared weapons of the second World War, began their deadly bombardment onto the advancing American troops. It was primarily an anti-aircraft gun, but the 88mm was adaptable to general artillery use against ground targets — in anti-infantry and anti-tank roles. The whole battlefield was suddenly alive with the never-ending, reverberating echoes of thunder. The ground beneath quaked mightily from the high-explosive shells targeting the hundreds of advancing Rainbow Division infantry soldiers as they charged forward.

Grandpa continued with his story.

"March 15th was one of the prettiest days; oh, it was beautiful. The sun was shining, the birds were singing.

"We went down the old rough road into a little village down there — Wimmenau. We got right in the middle of town, and I said something about it being such a beautiful morning, and one of the boys said, 'Beware the ides of March.'

"He hadn't no more than said that till WHEEEEEE … SWOOOHHH … BANG! They started throwing those 88 artillery shells in there — German 88 artillery. They were a deadly thing. And it was that way all day long.

"They hit our company commander's jeep right in the radiator and demolished it. He happened not to be in it at that time. They continued to throw them.

"Seemed like they were hunting for me. I went up to a truck, and there was an artillery shell that landed right on the other side of the truck and blowed the back tires out on it. I don't know how many fell right real close to me that day.

"We came on down below the village and started on down the road towards the next village, and I was following an M-1 tank. (We also had a bulldozer blade on the front of the tank. The Germans had big trees with dynamite, high explosives, around the butts of them. When they would retreat, they would set that off and the trees would fall over across the road, and it was a tangled mess for you to go through. That dozer would just back off and give a shove, and they'd break their way through with that thing.)

"I was following that tank, and there were several boys that got wounded. One boy had a piece of shrapnel that went right through his shoe and was sticking out at the bottom — a great big long piece of shrapnel that looked like a big butcher knife, except it was about an inch thick and about two inches wide."

Grandpa had our attention as he continued to describe what it was like when the Germans fired their 88mm artillery shells into the midst of the invading American troops. Under fire but undaunted, the men continued to move forward, toward the Westwall.

"There was one that fell right in front of the tank I was following. And then, in just a minute, why, I hear another one coming. Of course you hit the ground when you hear one of those things. You don't have to be told. It hit the ground behind me. Then I remembered in training they told us that if one went in front of you and one behind you, watch out for the middle one. I'd forgot about the tank, and I was thinking he was shooting at me.

"I heard the next one coming, and I just dived across the road — it was just a little old nine-foot road. I dived across head-down and threw my machine gun out in front of me. That shell went off, and I believe it would have fell right at my feet where I had been standing."

He was knocked unconscious by the blast.

"When I came to myself, my buddy was over me. I had this place here — it hit a blood vessel or something. There was blood all down my shirt and coat and all over my front, and they sent me back up there to a little wine cellar, where I went in for medical first aid."

He had been hit in the face and neck by shrapnel from the exploding German shell. He was helped by his battle buddy to a wine cellar that had been turned into a temporary medical aid station. There were still incoming rounds and explosions to deal with, but the cellar gave some protection to the wounded as they were being triaged and treated.

The medical personnel treating him gave him the option of going back, away from the front.

"I told them, 'No, I don't want to go back,' and we went on. That day, it was pretty rough. I wished a few times that I'd went back, but we went on."

We were curious as to who this battle buddy was he kept referring to. What was the name of this soldier who had been with him since he first stepped foot onto European soil and had continued with him through the snow covered Rhone River Valley and into combat?

"His last name was Kelley," he replied.

Of all the men he had encountered in the Army, he ended up with a brother-in-arms with the same name as his own little brother Kelly, who died at age 2 and lay in a grave in the mountains of Kentucky. Even though he spelled his last name slightly differ-ently, it was still, in essence, the same name they shared.

Within a few minutes, Blace was stitched, patched up, and put back in the fight. He and Kelley continued on through the shells and explosions.

"They were throwing artillery all day long, and then it began to get dark," Grandpa said.

Many of the engineers were being approached by the forward infantry soldiers and told to move up and into the front line for whatever skills were needed to assist in battle. After all, they were combat engineers.

They were initially kept busy clearing and repairing the roads of mines and craters, as well as trees felled by the Germans as they began to fall back and regroup. The roads were desperately needed for supplies as well as for advancing U.S. artillery as they continued to engage the enemy. The first three days of battle through the forest and mountains was extremely difficult and relied upon the skills of the U.S. soldiers, who were trained within their military occupational specialty code (or MOS).

This battle, through dense forest and enemy obstacles, was not only an infantryman's war, but also an engineer's war. The engineer's skills and training would play a key role in the aggressive pace needed to keep up the attack by clearing the way for others to follow.

These first few days of battle were just a foretaste of what lay ahead as the soldiers continued forward, as yet to encounter the Siegfried Line.

PHOTO ALBUM

An early family photograph. From left: J.E. Davis, Blace, Virginia "Vera," and Kelly.

Blace and his brother Kelly. He would never forget his little brother.

Private Blace Edward Davis in a training photograph from Camp Gruber, Oklahoma.

Private Blace Edward Davis, 42nd "Rainbow" Infantry Division.

The family home, Poplar Grove Road, Virginia.

The Davis children, photographed as Blace was leaving for the war. Back row, from left: Joanne, Blenda, Helen, and Richard. Front row: Judy (standing) and Janie. Note the service banner located in window behind the children.

Blace holding Judith "Judy" Elaine Davis and Jama Lee "Janie" Davis.

Blace with the weight of the world on his shoulders, one of the last photographs taken just prior to leaving his family for war.

Alma Lee (with child) and Blace. This photograph was taken while Blace was home on a pass, prior to his leaving the States in 1944. Their son, Edward "Eddie," would be born just a few months later.

Alma Lee Davis with children Eddie and Judy.

Blace Davis, Germany, 1945.

Germans pass by the broken shop window of a Jewish owned business that was destroyed during Kristallnacht. (Photo credit: United States Holocaust Memorial Museum, courtesy of National Archives and Records Administration, College Park. Date: November 10, 1938.)

Newly arrived prisoners, with shaven heads, stand at attention in their civilian clothes during a roll call in the Buchenwald concentration camp. Some still have their valises and other luggage with them. These prisoners were among the more than 10,000 German Jews who were arrested during the Kristallnacht pogrom (November 9-10, 1938) and sent to Buchenwald. Another 20,000 German Jews arrested at the same time were imprisoned in Dachau and Sachsenhausen. (Photo credit: United States Holocaust Memorial Museum, courtesy of Robert A. Schmuhl. Date: circa November 10, 1938.)

American soldiers view the Dachau death train. (Photo credit: United States Holocaust Memorial Museum, courtesy of K. L. Rabinoff-Goldman. Date: April 29, 1945.)

Dachau concentration camp. Young and old survivors in Dachau cheer approaching U.S. troops. (Photo credit: United States Holocaust Memorial Museum, courtesy of National Archives and Records Administration, College Park. Date: April 29, 1945.)

The Davis children pose for a family photograph. From left: Eddie, Judy, Janie, Helen, Blenda, Richard, and Joanne.

Davis family photograph. From left: Gary and Nancy (born after the war), Eddie, Judy, Janie, Helen, Blenda, Richard, and Joanne. Sitting: Alma and Blace.

My two brothers and I, taken at the time Grandpa was telling us about his war experiences. From left: Eddie, Mike, and me.

My grandparents' home. This was where Grandpa told us his war story.

My grandfather, Blace Edward Davis, as I'll always remember him.

THROUGH THE SIEGFRIED

"There is no death, only a change of worlds."
(Chief Sealth, Suquamish Native American tribe)

By day five of the attack, 42nd Rainbow Division continued to make gains and capture more ground. However, the advancing troops were about to encounter the numerous deadly German concrete pillboxes as they advanced toward the Siegfried Line near the town of Ludwigswinkel. This area was one of rugged terrain, heavily wooded, and filled with booby traps.

It was getting dark, and the forward infantry troops were still taking on fire from German forces just in front of their position. As Blace and Kelley were making their way up to the front, a German 88 artillery shell came crashing down through the canopy in a "tree burst." The men dived for cover. When they got up, they were surprised to see one of their buddies, last name of Steller, off in the distance and making his way forward. He had also somehow survived the ongoing shelling. The men were glad to see familiar faces, but the joy of that reunion would be short-lived.

The soldiers were now approaching the narrow Saarbach River. Just beyond the river lay the fortifications of the Siegfried Line. Rainbow Division's advance would now encounter what the Germans had for years been building: a vast array of elaborate, camouflaged pillbox fortifications, each linked with one another. These steel and concrete fortifications were precisely positioned in the surrounding terrain to allow for deadly crossfire from hundreds of German machine guns. These areas of crossfire, known as kill zones, were entirely covered by defensive fire, through which the attacking U.S. troops would have to advance. To get into Germany, Rainbow Division would first have to make it through this grim maze of pillbox fortifications and machine gun nests. The area before them seemed impenetrable.

"An officer came down — an infantry officer who had a few men with him," Grandpa said. "He told us that he wanted us to go with him. I carried an automatic machine gun. Our mission was to go around and get behind the ones that were cross-firing their machine guns on us. We were to go in there and run them out, root them out. The result was we ran right into them out there in the woods."

I remember Grandpa telling us, as we sat there in the basement, that the infantry officer quickly formed a squad and gave orders to each man. The captain had previously spied out what appeared to be a lone, camouflaged German machine gun nest off to one side that was the source of the crossfire. The officer was determined to take it by force.

The infantry squad advanced up the hill toward the enemy's location. As they began to receive fire, they fell to the ground and took cover behind logs and stumps, anything they could find, waiting for the Nazi machine-gunner to reload when he ran out of ammunition.

As they got set to make their advance, two of the men laid

down a barrage of nonstop automatic weapon fire directly to the front of the machine gun nest — just like they had been trained. The infantry officer likely hoped this would allow him some cover as he and the other men made their way around through the woods, approaching both sides of the nest. They planned on blowing it up with grenades.

Grandpa said this seemed to be a good plan, but they were not expecting the Germans to flee the nest. He and Steller were busy climbing the hill hurrying to get in position at the back of the other side — behind the crossfire and away from the forward action. Before Grandpa could get set with his .50-caliber "Ma Deuce" machine gun, the Germans, realizing what was happening, stormed out of the back side of the nest and began firing on my grandfather's position. One of Grandpa's greatest fears was coming true: He couldn't get his weapon in shooting position fast enough.

"We run right into them," said Grandpa. "We hit the ground. I never did fire my gun; I didn't see anything to shoot at. Steller was lying right next to me, and I glanced at him and he motioned, and I noticed that the German machine gun fire was bouncing off that tree. You could see the bark jumping off above his head.

"He was lying there with his foot on a trip wire that was tied to a hand grenade on the side of another tree. He was afraid to move his foot because they fixed them up with a pressure release. If you cut it, it would blow off. If you pulled it, it would go off. He was afraid to move his foot, afraid to cut it. He was afraid of what the result would be. But he got it off some way or another. That thing would have killed us all if it had went off."

Grandpa told us that he and Steller remained low to the

ground as bullets zipped in their direction from all sides. Their buddies were returning fire as they lay prone on the ground under the crossfire. He later learned that one of the men had crawled around the opposite side of the nest, sprang forward from his position and tossed a grenade. As suddenly as it began, it was over. The Germans were dead, and the captain had succeeded in taking his first machine gun nest. But the men were still in trouble.

Off in the distance were numerous pillboxes that appeared to be about one hundred yards apart. The number of pillboxes was more than what intelligence had reported. Grandpa said the Germans were bound to have had very good observation of what had just happened as they, too, continued to fire upon the men. Realizing this, the captain ordered the men to fall back.

While we sat there in the basement, Grandpa got up and added another log to the wood stove. He looked outside through the basement window as the sun was setting.

"The Germans would usually launch counterattacks after nightfall," he said. "These attacks would begin with a lot of shouting and talking. The boys and I began to hear German chatter off in the distance, from the Siegfried Line fortifications. We were worried that we could be outmanned and outgunned. Our squad moved back to regroup with the others and took shelter for the night in a German house near the northern edge of France."

There would be no sleeping for these men, as their adrenaline continued to course through their bodies. It would be early the next morning before they joined back up with their group.

The next day, on March 21, 1945, Allied support aircraft, including P-47 Thunderbolts, dive-bombed and pounded the German fortifications, along with supporting artillery bombardment. The Americans hunkered down in their foxholes as they watched the spectacle play out in front of their eyes. Grandpa told us that he had never witnessed bombardment of such magnitude.

"It appeared that the entire Siegfried Line was alive with fire," he said.

That afternoon, the 42nd Infantry Division resumed its advance and found that most of the Germans who had previously manned the Siegfried Line were not even putting up a fight. In fact, some of them had already started to run. There were still a few snipers and machine guns to deal with, though.

The enemy was in the process of trying to regroup. Now was the opportunity to catch them on the run and cut them off before they succeeded in their escape.

Grandpa said that Rainbow's forward observers, known as fire support specialists, realized what was happening as the Germans fell back, and immediately targeted the locations of the fleeing enemy with artillery bombardment. At the same time, P-47 Thunderbolt aircraft swarmed overhead as they assisted in the offensive attack. Whole columns of German soldiers were wiped out, as Rainbow Division continued one of its biggest artillery bombardments of the war. The roads and hill sides were littered with enemy dead.

The remaining Germans who had previously manned the Siegfried Line were surrendering everywhere. The survivors threw down their weapons and gave themselves up. Within twenty-four hours of its initial breaking through the Westwall,

Rainbow Division had taken more that 2,000 prisoners.

The combat engineers still had work to do. They began to set off explosive charges, destroying many of the remaining Siegfried Line fortifications. This was done so that the fortifications could never again be used by the Germans.

During those first days of battle, the soldiers had advanced more that fifteen miles through the Hardt Mountains and into German territory.

Grandpa told us that Rainbow Division had a Jewish chaplain, who held the first Jewish religious services during Passover in the town of Dahn. This was the first of such services to be conducted in that region of Germany since the Nazis had taken power.

For now, 42nd Rainbow Division had a taste of victory. Grandpa said that he and his buddies were thankful to be alive, having made it through the Siegfried Line. He also said he was amazed that on the other side of the Siegfried Line, there was not a single German admitting to be a Nazi.

This victory was short-lived, as orders were soon issued from Command to continue onward into the very heart of Germany. The division was ordered to proceed across the Rhine River, and then eastward.

The men were soon to find out that the German army staged a rear guard action, briefly defending towns from the advancing American troops, then retreating to the next to regroup as civilians joined in the fight. They would also be up against Hitler's feared SS troops — a first-rate paramilitary unit whose men were known to profess undying loyalty to their *führer*.

It was at this point in his story that Grandpa also mentioned the word *"Volkssturm."*

"What does that mean?" my oldest brother asked.

"It means 'people's storm,'" he replied. "Not only did we have to fight against Hitler's SS, but also against fanatical civilians. Some were only teenagers."

Grandpa told us that the *Volkssturm* was a national militia established by the Nazi party on the orders of Hitler. Civilians previously deemed unfit — those recovering from wounds and those who were overage, as well as the underage- members of the Hitler Youth — were drafted by the Nazis during the last months of the war. Desperate Nazis even drafted German women and girls into the auxiliaries of the *Volkssturm*.

Grandpa continued: "On Easter Sunday morning, we were up on top of a big hill, and the boys wanted me to read them the Easter story. And I was reading it, Matthew and Luke. I was reading the resurrection story, and the captain came up in his jeep and said, "I want two volunteers to go with me.

"Everybody dropped their heads. That was one thing they wouldn't do — they never volunteered for anything. And he said, 'Okay, Davis — you and Steller come on.' He volunteered us."

"Where was the captain taking you to?" my cousin asked.

"Wurzburg," he replied.

On Easter Sunday, the Rainbow regiments loaded their equipment and supplies onto jeeps and trucks and began crossing the Rhine River.

In order to get across the Rhine, the engineers had constructed a floating bridge known as a pontoon bridge. They used barges or boats' pontoons to support the bridge deck. This type of bridge had been used in war as far back as ancient times — even by the Roman legions.

As the men crossed the Rhine River near the city of Worms, Blace got his first real glimpse of the destruction that the Air Force could inflict. Across the landscape, not a house or building was left standing. Only rubble remained. This would become an all too familiar sight for the men of Rainbow Division as they continued to move deeper into enemy territory.

They were now headed to the River Main, just east of Wertheim. From there they would continue their push eastward toward Wurzburg, where the Nazis were trying to regroup. There was soon a feeling of dread when the men learned that the Germans planned on putting up a fight in what was left of that city, known by locals as "the grave on the River Main."

Rapid Advance

"The art of war is simple enough. Find out where your enemy is. Get at him as soon as you can. Strike him as hard as you can, and keep moving on."

(Ulysses S. Grant)

Grandpa pulled out a dust-covered German postcard from the bottom of his gray wall locker. He passed the postcard around as we huddled near the warmth of the Mama Bear wood stove. It had the Third Reich symbol stamped onto the back of it. The postcard was later interpreted and found to have been written by a German soldier congratulating his comrade on his recent advancement in rank.

Grandpa told us that as he and Steller rode in the back of the jeep eastward toward the city of Wurzburg, the captain, who was sitting up front, mentioned why he needed volunteers. Up ahead they were to join in helping a fellow group of combat engineers. Many of the Germans had retreated from the Siegfried Line and gone into Wurzburg, one of the oldest cities in southern Germany. In their retreat, the Germans had blown three bridges spanning the River Main and leading into the city.

Blace was told that a group of Rangers had already crossed the river shortly before dawn in order to secure a bridgehead into

Wurzburg. He also learned that assault boats had been moved up to the front lines to assist the Rangers and supporting infantry troops. The captain needed volunteers to move up to the front and assist the other combat engineers with their rapid bridge construction for the arrival of more infantry troops who would cross the river with their vehicles and equipment.

The city of Wurzburg was the most damaged place Grandpa had ever seen. He tried as best he could to describe what it was like.

"It was littered with bomb craters and destroyed buildings. The whole city lay in ruin," he said. "As far as the eye could see was nothing but piles upon piles of busted bricks, concrete, and shells of buildings. It was all that was left."

A strategic bombing campaign by the Allies had essentially turned the city into a heap of rubble. The British Royal Air Force bomber group that carried out the attack was known as the No. 5 group.

On the evening of March 16, 1945, just three weeks prior to the 42nd Infantry Rainbow Division's arrival in Wurzburg, Avro Lancaster bombers of No. 5 group launched from runways west of London. The bombers took a winding route, deceiving German air defenses in order to reach their target. Air raid alarms sounded, as thousands below scrambled to take cover. Overhead, 225 Lancasters and 11 Mosquito combat-ready aircraft of the No. 5 group began their deadly bombardment.

Grandpa told us he learned later that Bomber Command had shifted its focus to the morale of the enemy population. They carried out massive carpet bombings in a path of destruction that the advancing troops would follow as they continued to move deeper into German territory.

The British Royal Air Force had dropped incendiary bombs on the city of Wurzburg, killing an estimated 5,000 people. Almost ninety percent of the buildings in the city were destroyed. The raid lasted less than twenty minutes.

Departing bomber crews were reported to have seen the glare of the burning city from more than 240 kilometers away.

Even with this amount of destruction, the men of the 42nd Infantry Division were about to learn that the Germans, with fanatical zeal, still planned to defend the city of Wurzburg.

Grandpa said he could remember sitting in the back seat of the jeep, looking up ahead on the road they were traveling. Coming into view, just across the river, was a huge fortress known as the Marienburg Castle. It, too, had been severely damaged by the Allies' bombing raid. At the base of the fortress lay the River Main, which separated the advancing troops from the city of Wurzburg. The Germans were firing from the other side with rifles and 20-mm artillery. As the men jumped from the jeep to take cover, Blace noticed something strange across the river: The Germans had painted two words in large white letters on the front wall of the castle.

"What did the words say?" my cousin asked.

"*Heil* Hitler!" Grandpa said. "The Nazis were fanatics."

The men joined in with the other combat engineers, who were busy unloading bridge-building equipment. Grandpa said he remembered the very first words out of the officer's mouth: "Keep your eyes open. There are snipers all over the place!"

Grandpa told us it was not just German military snipers, but also civilian snipers, that the advancing troops had to deal with.

By the time Blace arrived at the river's edge, the Rangers had already made the crossing undetected. But the engineer assault boats were now engaged in transporting infantry troops across the water, under heavy fire. He also saw a soldier take a direct hit from an enemy sniper who had fired from across the river.

As Grandpa continued with his story, he stood up from where he was sitting and began to clap his hands. He looked straight into our faces and, with a strong commanding voice, said, "There's no time to waste! Let's go! Let's go!"

Rainbow infantry troops were arriving by the hundreds, and those men needed to get across the river as soon as possible to join in the assault on Wurzburg. Over the river was one of the bridges the Germans had blown. It was a partially bombed-out bridge that had large statues of lions. He said it was known locally as the Lyons Bridge, but the real name was Ludwig's Bridge. The engineers quickly estimated it would take at least twenty-four hours to complete a temporary structure over the bombed-out section that would be strong enough to allow the arriving troops and heavy vehicles to cross.

On the other side of the river, the Rangers of the 2nd Battalion, along with men from the 222nd Infantry, persisted in their assault. They continued with the goal of securing the bridgehead so that the other infantry regiments could cross.

The captain and other engineer officers quickly came up with a plan. They would begin three projects simultaneously. One project was to construct a raft and ferry system, which could be pulled across the river by ropes. It could be completed within a few hours. That would be followed by construction of a pontoon treadway bridge — another type of floating bridge that used floats or shallow-draft boats to support a continuous deck for military troops and light-vehicle travel. Even though the buoyancy of this type of bridge limited the maximum loads the vehicles could carry, these two bridges would allow some of the advancing infantry, along with weapons, ammunition, jeeps and signal equipment, to get across.

The third project was to immediately begin work on a Bailey bridge — a portable, prefabricated truss bridge. It would span the missing section of Ludwig's Bridge, which was blown apart by the Germans when they retreated into Wurzburg. Developed by the British during World War II, this type of bridge saw extensive use by U.S. military engineering units. It could be completed in less than 24 hours and could be used for massive troop movement across the river as well as for heavy vehicles, trucks and, most importantly, tanks.

Grandpa told us that one of the best advantages of a Bailey bridge was that it required no special tools or heavy equipment to assemble. Its unconstructed pieces were small and light enough to be carried in trucks and lifted into place by hand. The Bailey bridge could be constructed without the use of a crane.

The men completed the Bailey bridge before dawn on the morning of April 4. Foot troops of the 232nd Infantry regiment crossed into the area already being cleared by the Rangers of the 2nd Battalion and 222nd Infantry, thereby renewing the attack into Wurzburg.

That day, Rainbow Division was engaged in what some described as the most bitter resistance they had encountered as a complete unit. Grandpa again reminded us that not only were they fighting against German soldiers, but also against armed civilians known as the *Volkssturm* — or the people's militia — many of whom were trained to fight to the death to save their homeland.

Many of these individuals carried a *Panzerfaust*, a high-explosive projectile stored in a long tube with folding rear sight and trigger. These types of weapons required little skill to operate. The explosive projectiles, capable of penetrating the armor of any fighting vehicle, were being fired indiscriminately into the advancing American troops. Also, snipers persisted in deadly weapon fire from hidden locations.

As Rainbow Division continued forward, they were unknowingly being led into a trap. Invisible to the naked eye were tunnels that the Germans had tug beneath the rubble-filled city. The retreating enemy would use the tunnels to sneak up behind the advancing troops and reengage the fight. The U.S. soldiers now found themselves being attacked from the rear — some in hand-to-hand combat — as darkness began to fall on April 5.

This counterattack by the Nazis was soon met by the overwhelming force of Rainbow Division as it countered, inflicting heavy casualties on the enemy, who had made it to just within 100 yards of the Bailey bridge.

The U.S. soldiers regrouped and continued to push through the city, systematically searching for enemy resistance in tunnels, cellars and what was left of any buildings.

Grandpa noted that more than 2,500 enemy combatants

were captured in the taking of the city. The battle of Wurzburg was over. Many of the defenders of the city had fled northward along the River Main for Schweinfurt. The men of Rainbow Division would now head north into one of the most important industrial cities in Germany.

As fast as the men of 142nd Engineer Combat Battalion had completed the raft and ferry system, the temporary pontoon treadway bridge, and the Bailey bridge, it was time once again to move to the front for the next assault. They were needed immediately to begin construction of a treadway bridge across the River Main at Nordheim, fifteen miles south of Schweinfurt, so that Combat Command could cross the river and cut the Germans' escape route to the east.

These ongoing engineering feats, completed while in combat and at times under direct enemy fire, were proving crucial in maintaining the speed and tempo of forward movement. This ongoing rapid advance of 42nd Infantry Rainbow Division into Germany was likened to a meteor tearing through the atmosphere.

Up ahead of the division, throughout the towns and villages, the enemy had prepared defensive positions. These positions were strategically placed along the planned route that the invading American troops were expected to take on their way to Schweinfurt. Each town and village had small groups of enemy fighters lying in wait. In the city of Schweinfurt, some 5,000 German soldiers and *Volkssturm* militia were given direct orders from the German SS commander to remain and fight until the very last. There was also intelligence that reported that SS soldiers had hung three men who wanted to surrender to the Americans.

The division continued to push northward toward the city of Schweinfurt, once again encountering German infantry and shelling from their deadly 88mm artillery. Rainbow's forward observers reported that in front of the division was nothing but an open flat area that offered no protection from the incoming German artillery. If they continued with their current plan of attack, they would pay for it in thousands of American lives.

Poplar Grove

"You know that place between sleep and awake, the place where you can still remember dreaming? That's where I'll always love you. That's where I'll be waiting."
                                  (Peter Pan, created by Sir J.M. Barrie)

It was an evening in the second week of April 1945. In a small wood frame house in Virginia sat Blace's wife, Alma. She gazed out the front window at the setting sun and gently rocked her five-month-old son, Eddie, in her arms. He had been born while Blace was training in the States before leaving for Europe.

Next to her, fast asleep, were her two youngest daughters, Jama Lee (Janie), three years old, and Judith Elaine (Judy), who was two years old. Alma could not help but to think back to the last time she saw her husband before he left for the war. He had received a seventy-two-hour pass before leaving the States. She had photos of him in full dress uniform with the family, and she remembered him waving as he departed from home.

Suddenly the back door flew open. In through the door ran her oldest son, Richard, who was ten years old, as well as daughters Joanne, Helen and Blenda. They had just finished up with their chores. The family quickly gathered in the living room as Richard turned on the radio. Television would not arrive until the early 1950s. Radio and newspaper were the only sources of news in those days.

Grandma got up from where she was sitting and handed Eddie over to Joanne. She then pulled out a map in preparation for the upcoming war news. Edward R. Murrow and Gabriel Heatter were two announcers they would often hear.

Richard could recall his mother waiting to painstakingly mark and color the map as she listened for any information as to the troop movements and the location of 42nd Infantry Rainbow Division. This was a way to chart the locations where her husband had been and was likely heading as the war continued. As they watched their mother work on the map, the Davis children were actually learning more about Europe than they ever would learn in school.

"Sometimes we would hear that dad's outfit was engaged in house-to-house fighting in a certain city and that civilians were firing from buildings at our troops," Richard said. "Then we would hear of someone we knew who was killed, or someone missing in action, and that would add to our anxiety."

Raising seven children while their father was away in service was where the real war was being fought. Throughout that first year Alma, was known for her resourceful personality, for never losing her sense of humor, and especially for her love for her husband and family.

Alma was also fortunate during that time to have some kind neighbors and friends who assisted her family in their time of need. Mr. Rector and his wife, Eldean, would make a habit of checking on the Davis household every week to see if they needed anything. Ms. Mayes, who lived across the road, would help with laundry and housework, as would Lizzie Moser.

My uncle Richard also noted in a letter: "Lizzie Moser was a wonderful friend to Mom while Dad was away. She would work like a Trojan — washing, ironing, canning, sewing … just anything to help out. She spent many days working at the house."

These two women were also there for support when Alma gave birth to her son, Eddie, at home, while Blace was away in service. Dr. Virgil Cox, the hometown medical doctor, performed the delivery.

Those war years were never to be forgotten by the children. They worked and contributed as best they could to the war effort. Each child eagerly helped, knowing that their dad was away, fighting overseas. At Poplar Grove School, the children would collect scrap metal. They would also gather milkweed or "silkweed" pods for use in manufacturing raw materials for life jackets and parachutes. Victory gardens, gas and food rationing, scrap drives and salvage collections were commonplace in conserving resources for the war effort.

That evening, the children listened to the radio announcer's breaking news: Rainbow Division was reported to have fought its way to the outer defenses of the city of Schweinfurt, the center of the Nazi ball bearing industry. An air bombardment of the city was called in due to the amount of German 88mm artillery encountered by U.S. troops on the ground. Reports were that bomber crews had flown three raids over the city, and a total of 192 planes had dropped their bomb loads on the city's defenses. Rainbow Division was reported to have struck into the city. No further information was available at the time.

Times like this kept the family on edge. Not knowing what was happening to the troops on the ground was the worst part. All the family could do was to hope and pray.

The children found some comfort in knowing that they were not alone by hanging a service banner in the window of their small home. Such a banner was proudly hung for the entire world to see. The banner had a white field with a red border and contained a single blue star, representing their father as he fought in the war. Many such banners hung in the windows along Poplar Grove Road during that time and were dotted throughout the landscape.

Unfortunately, as the war progressed, so did the casualties. One day as Alma was traveling home from Mt. Vale Church with her children, she noticed something that caused her to pause. Off in a distant field, across from the dirt road where they were walking, sat a small house with all of its shades pulled down. The service banner so proudly hung there had been replaced. The new banner contained a single blue-bordered gold star, a simple, cherished symbol indicating that their service member had died while in combat. For that family, the war had come to an abrupt and horrible end. Not wanting to add to her children's anxiety, Alma kept this observation to herself and continued for home.

A few days later, Alma's sister-in-law and friend, Pauline, had received word that her brother, PFC Louis Eli Winesett, Jr., had been killed in action. He was posthumously awarded the Silver Star medal, the nation's third highest valorous combat decoration, for his actions taken before his death on April 17, 1945, in Monterumici, Italy. His platoon was said to have entered battle against the Germans early that morning and had become trapped. Even though he was already wounded, he reportedly climbed up a hill to draw the shooting in his direction so that his group could get out. He was killed in the process, laying down his life to save the lives of others.

The whole community of Poplar Grove was impacted by the ever increasing news of service members who would not be returning home from the war. Families were constantly on edge, wondering if they, too, would be the next to hear that their father, husband, son, or brother had been killed in combat.

Mt. Vale United Methodist Church was an anchor for the community during that period, a gathering place for friends and family, a place that offered comfort, support, and fellowship in a time of uncertainty.

Undesirable Elements

"Who has inflicted this upon us? Who has made us Jews
different from all other people? Who has allowed us to
suffer so terribly up till now? It is God that has made
us as we are, but it will be God, too, who will raise us
up again. If we hear all this suffering and if there are
still Jews left, when it is over, then Jews, instead of being
doomed, will be held up as an example."

(Anne Frank)

The factories of Schweinfurt produced most of Nazi Germany's desperately needed ball bearings. It became a target of Allied strategic bombing during World War II in an effort to cripple aircraft and tank production. A few years prior, it had been bombed several times during Operation Pointblank. Bombing also included the Second Raid on Schweinfurt on October 14, 1943, called Black Thursday because of the enormous loss of Allied aircraft and lives, and Big Week in February 1944. Hitler had made restoration of ball bearing production a high priority, as such items were necessary to keep his war machines operational.

Over a year later, Schweinfurt found itself surrounded by the men of 42nd Infantry Rainbow Division, who were poised to attack. Prior to their attack, their commander, General Collins, chose to use air power to soften up the Germans' artillery defenses. A total of 192 planes were called in, flying three raids over the city and dropping their ordnance onto enemy positions below.

During the night of April 10, 1945, patrols from the 242nd Infantry would be the first to move out across the large open plain in front of what was left of the bombed-out city. The patrols would lead the 242nd Infantry regiment in its approach directly to the center of Schweinfurt. The other parts of Rainbow Division would split with the 232nd Infantry, engaging the enemy at the north part of Schweinfurt, while the 222nd Infantry would engage the southern region. The 12th Armored Division would also engage the enemy if he tried to escape eastward. This plan of attack essentially surrounded the city.

Urban warfare was very different from combat out in the open, such as what Blace had encountered while going through the Siegfried Line back in March. What complicated matters most in urban warfare was the presence of civilians as well as the complexity of the urban terrain. In addition, the German SS had prepared a defense made up of groups of retreating enemy — just as they had done in Wurzburg — with instructions to remain and fight along the roads, strategic high ground, towns and cities.

Blace had seen some of this in what remained of Wurzburg, and now he was facing it again in Schweinfurt. He could only imagine the loss of life the U.S. Army might have experienced had it not been for the Western Allies' intensive aerial bombardment, which went ahead of them as they continued their final assault on the city. Despite the destruction, he knew that the Germans' will to put up a fight seemed relentless.

Blace and other members of the combat engineers now saw the battered city of Schweinfurt, which lay in ruin around them. Once again, the air bombardment prior to their entry had achieved a devastating effect, but the famed ball bearing factories were still operational. Still, their production was only about 30 percent of capacity, as the factories were manned by slave laborers from concentration camps, people whom Hitler had classified as "undesirable elements." As the infantrymen captured the plants, the surviving slave laborers came out of bomb shelters and joyfully hugged their liberators.

The capture of Schweinfurt took three days, from April 9 through April 11, 1945. Blace, along with many of the combat engineers, were ordered to assist with mop up operations. They followed behind Sherman bulldozer tanks, which cleared paths through the rubble in what was left of the city's streets. The men then spread out behind the tanks, searching for any remaining enemy.

"There's nothing spectacular about a mop up operation. It's typically the forgotten phase of any battle," he said.

In a mop up operation, everything is passed off as being peaceful and quiet. That sounds very nice, except that men continue to die in skirmishes waged in destroyed city buildings, bunkers and tunnels. It remained a very dangerous part of the war.

Rainbow Division rounded up more than 3,000 prisoners from the city of Schweinfurt and its surrounding area. Since leaving Wurzburg, the division had captured more that 6,680 German soldiers.

It was also at this time that the Army received word of President Franklin D. Roosevelt's death. He had passed away on April 12, 1945, as the men were fighting in Schweinfurt. On April 13, the men of the 242nd officially gathered, among the bomb-blasted ruins, for a brief memorial service for their commander in chief.

That same day, Rainbow Division was ordered to proceed southeast and prepare to attack the cities of Furth and Nuremberg. Once again, the Nazis were expected to put up a fight, especially in defending the city of Nuremberg, where Nazism was known to have flourished among its people.

STRONGHOLDS OF NAZISM

First they came for the Socialists, and I did not speak out —
Because I was not a Socialist.
Then they came for the Trade Unionists, and I did not
  speak out —
Because I was not a Trade Unionist.
Then they came for the Jews, and I did not speak out —
Because I was not a Jew.
Then they came for me —
And there was no one left to speak for me.
                    (Martin Niemöller 1892-1984)

Our parents were still upstairs visiting with Grandma. Grandpa seemed content with continuing with his story. He opened up the stove door and added another split log to the fire. A few embers escaped, dancing across the basement's concrete floor as he shut the door.

"There's one more thing I want to show you," he said.

He reached overhead and pulled on a string cord, turning on an additional light. Reaching back into his wall locker, he pulled out a small dagger enclosed in a metal sheath with leather strap.

He removed the dagger from its protective sheath. It was a Hitler Youth knife, its handle emblazoned with a German swastika. The overhead light glistened across its sharp steel blade reflecting the words "*Blut und Ehre!*"

"What do those words mean, Grandpa?"

"It means 'Blood and Honor!'" he said.

He explained to us that Hitler believed the future of Nazi Germany was its children. For years before the war, such children were lured and recruited by attractive activities for young men and boys. There were many children who joined the Hitler Youth, and they were brainwashed by the Nazi party system with their beliefs and racism.

In Hitler's Germany, the people saw and heard only what Hitler wanted them to see and hear. Books — including children's books that did not line up with the Nazi regime — were outlawed and burned. Those books were replaced by ones demeaning the Jews while at the same time glorifying the Aryan race — a so-called superior strain of humanity, or "master race." Nazis claimed to be direct descendants of the Aryan race.

Grandpa said it was in Nuremberg (spelled "Nurnberg" in German) that Hitler would hold huge Nazi propaganda rallies. He said that these rallies drew hundreds of thousands of Nazi Party members and spectators, including hundreds of foreign journalists who covered the rallies.

I remember him telling us that the German people would get caught up in listening to rousing speeches by "the *führer*." He said it was in Nuremberg, during these rallies, that Hitler announced new Nazi directions to the massed crowds, such as the racist Nuremberg Laws that were put into effect against the Jews. Grandpa noted that such laws did not come from nowhere.

"They come from lawmakers or lawgivers," he said. "Hitler and his Nazis were the ones making up such laws."

The Nuremberg Laws deprived Jews living in Germany of their German citizenship. At that time the Jews found themselves confined to the status of "subjects." By controlling the nation's laws, Hitler gained control of the nation's agenda.

Grandpa said that prior to the war, one of the largest rallies ever held took place at Nuremberg. He said it had in attendance more than 700,000 members of Nazi Party organizations and that more than 80,000 Hitler Youths marched into the German stadium of Nuremberg, performing military-style parade maneuvers. A few months later, in November 1938, *Kristallnacht* occurred.

"What is *Kristallnacht*?" my cousin asked.

"It means 'Night of Broken Glass,'" Grandpa said.

Kristallnacht occurred when Nazi storm troopers, the SS, and Hitler Youths attacked Jews throughout Germany. Jews were beaten. Their shops and synagogues had their windows smashed and contents destroyed. Police and crowds stood by as the attacks occurred. Thousands of Jewish men were hauled off to concentration camps, including Dachau, Buchenwald, and Sachsenhausen. Their places of business and worship were looted and destroyed and had the word "JUDE" painted on the walls. From that time on, all Jews had to wear the Star of David.

In many towns, Jews were forbidden to purchase food or conduct any type of business. Deprived of their livelihoods, many faced starvation. Hitler's Nuremberg Laws were designed to remove Jews from their status as human beings. Jews could be killed without fear of reprisal. With these laws in place, the

German SS troops began to exterminate Jews. With the creation of such laws, Germany started down a long, dark road — in essence molding itself into Hitler's own image.

"Don't you ever follow something or someone just because everybody else is doing it," Grandpa said.

He also told us there was supposed to be another rally held at Nuremberg during the final months of 1939, the so-called Rally of Peace. That rally never happened. One day prior to the planned date, on September 1, Germany began an offensive against Poland, igniting World War II.

Six years after Germany's invasion into Poland, the men of Rainbow Division were poised for another attack against Hitler's forces. Their target this time would be Furth, the western third of the Nazi shrine city of Nuremberg.

Grandpa said that the attack on Furth would be swift, hopefully catching the Germans off guard before they had a chance to rally a defense. Rainbow Division would attack from the west, 3rd Infantry from the north, 45th Infantry from the east, and 12th Armored Division along with the 4th Infantry from the south. It would require five divisions to take this fanatically defended section of enemy territory.

Just outside of Furth lay the town of Neustadt, on the Aisch River. The Germans had already moved soldiers into the area, knowing the advancing Rainbow Division would pass through on its way to Nuremberg. Their plan failed, however, as they were not strong enough to withstand a division advance. Still, the Germans inflicted some casualties on Rainbow Division. The division, though battered, quickened its pace as it headed deeper into enemy territory.

In the city of Furth were approximately 7,500 German troops from various units, as well as *Volkssturm* militia, who had been fleeing before Rainbow's advance. Roadblocks and barriers had been set. The Germans had also blown bridges leading into the city. They expected the Americans to arrive and begin their attack on April 19, at which time they were planning to defend Furth as best they could before retreating to Nuremberg to stage a last-ditch effort there. Mass confusion was spreading throughout the city, as preparations to battle the Americans were hurriedly being executed. The Germans thought they had at least another day or two to prepare for Rainbow Division's arrival.

Grandpa told us that General Collins always wanted his men in Rainbow Division to be aggressive when they went into battle. That aggressiveness had now paid off. Covering more ground than anyone believed possible, they struck the city of Furth on the morning of April 18, catching the Germans by complete surprise.

In their confusion, the enemy defenders battled desperately, but Rainbow Division continued its aggressive, systematic attack, taking out defenders with small-arms fire and artillery. The men of Rainbow Division cleared building after building of enemy combatants before they had a chance to carry out their planned escape to Nuremberg. In the end, more than 5,000 Germans surrendered. Grandpa said he could still remember seeing the Germans surrendering everywhere in the city.

"We would approach the Germans with our weapons drawn and signal for them to put their arms up in the air as they dropped their guns," he said. "We immediately frisked them for any hidden weapons. Everywhere you looked, knives and guns would hit the ground. Anybody who wanted a German knife or dagger got one. As combat engineers, we would use them as utility tools. Spoils of war."

Outposts of the Redoubt Area

"War is cruelty. There is no use trying to reform it. The crueler it is, the sooner it will be over."

(William Tecumseh Sherman)

Grandpa told us the relentless, aggressive pace of Rainbow Division continued to speed up the farther they got into Germany. The loss of sleep, along with the mental and emotional strain of continued combat, was also taking a toll on their bodies. Supplies to the front lines were becoming limited as they continued deep into Hitler's backyard.

"Many of us had lost fifteen to twenty pounds, which was not uncommon for soldiers in combat. We were down to K rations, which was just the basic ration of food," he said.

"We were told by Command to head south after our assault on Furth. There were rumors that the Nazis were going to make a last stand, known as a redoubt, around Berchtesgaden, Hitler's mountaintop home in Bavaria."

Rainbow Division was to engage the enemy near the Danube River, just south of their present location. As the soldiers of Rainbow Division made their way, they were accompanied on their left side by the 106th Calvary Group. On their right side was the 12th Armored Division.

They would be heading directly toward the vicinity of the German redoubt area. This location, an area located in the Alps, was where Adolph Hitler was rumored to be planning a last stand with his German SS. The fear was that if it were true, the Nazis could possibly reorganize there and continue with the war.

Throughout the territory before them, the Nazi SS had gathered what was left of stragglers from various army units and positioned them along certain crossroads and high ground. They were ordered to defend until the last against the advancing Americans. Solid as some were, the Germans were no match for an entire division of Rainbow soldiers, who continued to fight their way forward.

As they neared the town of Donauworth, preparations made by the Germans indicated that they were going to put up a fight. The bridge on the outskirts of Donauworth, across the Danube River, was one of the outposts of the redoubt defense area. The Germans had heavily mined the roads leading into this area.

Blace's engineer battalion immediately began sweeping the roads for mines in preparation for tanks to assist in the attack from the 20th Armored Division's 27th Tank Battalion. Small-arms fire and some artillery began to fall upon the men in a deadly exchange with the Germans. For almost two days straight, there was little to no sleep for these men.

By morning on April 25, the 27th Tank Battalion, attached to Rainbow Division, had reached the town of Donauworth and, without hesitation, immediately struck the German front, leading the attack. The city was heavily defended by approximately 700 Germans, most of whom were SS troops. The Germans were taken by complete surprise when they heard the rumble of tanks approaching their area. They had expected a slower advance by a division on foot.

It was around this time in his story that Grandpa made a sobering statement. He did not expect to make it back from the war alive. He said he had already accepted the grim reality that the odds of survival were not in his favor, especially in light of what he was being exposed to on a daily basis as he and the men continued in combat. He was witnessing death on a daily basis. Death was all around him.

He told us that as he thought back to those times in battle, even though he did not know it at the time, he was actually on the doorstep of God's holy dwelling place. Just one heartbeat away from entering eternity.

As the 27th Tank Battalion led the attack, Blace followed the tanks on foot as he and the men pushed forward as ordered. The German SS continued to direct artillery and small-arms fire on the approaching soldiers. At the same time, there were German soldiers fleeing across an open field on the opposite side of the river, where they continued to fire their weapons on the advancing American troops. The 27th Tank Battalion, realizing what was happening, immediately rotated the turrets of their tanks and opened fire on the enemy forces. Infantrymen following from Rainbow Division also fired their machine guns, leaving the ground littered with enemy dead.

As the 27th Tank Battalion entered the town, several tanks exploded from huge mines hidden in the road. This was only a momentary delay for Rainbow's advance; they continued forward through enemy fire and tangled debris. The Germans also blew the bridge behind them with a powerful explosive charge pre-planted on the bridge. It was their only means of escape from the town. The battle continued. The remaining hardened SS troops had no thoughts of surrender and decided to fight to the death when they blew the bridge. Soon they were engaged in house-to-house fighting, which lasted more than six hours. In the end, Rainbow Division captured the town and took only seventeen prisoners alive.

This attack, led by Rainbow's 20th Armored Division, 27th Tank Battalion, was key in securing the upcoming crossing of the Danube River.

THE HARDEST PART

*"If we wish to live and to bequeath life to our offspring, if
we believe that we are to pave the way to the future, then
we must first of all not forget."*
(Professor Ben Zion Dinur, Yad Vashem, 1956)

Rainbow Division was one of the first American units to reach the
Danube. It immediately began its crossing with orders to begin
the drive for Munich some 100 miles away. Blace and the men of
Company B 142nd Engineer Battalion manned assault boats as
they began the task of getting the infantrymen across the river.
Once safely across, Rainbow Division continued south for two
miles before turning and heading for the swift-flowing Lech River,
located four miles away.

Grandpa told us that he and several of his fellow engineers
were called up to the front by an infantry officer to where the
232nd Infantry was located east of the town of Genderkingen.
They were needed to assess a partially destroyed bridge that the
Nazis had left crippled when they retreated across the Lech River.

"As we arrived," he said, "we had to take cover immediately,
as a few Germans were still in the process of directing small-arms
fire on our location from across the river. The officer crouched
down beside us, also taking cover, with his hand on top of his

helmet. He asked us if the partially sunken bridge could be made passable.

"We could see that portions of the large steel bridge had been blown by the Nazis and had sunk just below the waterline. We made the determination that it could be made passable if we were able to get a few assault boats and planking in just the right places where the structure was under the water. It was getting dark, and we would use the cover of darkness to go out and begin the repairs.

"As darkness fell, we began to approach the structure in the assault boats. The Germans must have figured out what we were doing, as they likely could hear us with our boats and equipment. They began to fire at random from across the river, hoping to hit someone in the darkness. We continued with our mission and moved out onto the bridge while bullets zipped by us in the water. We began the repairs. Several of my buddies were hit by the enemy's small-arms fire."

Blace's task was completed just before midnight. Infantry troops crossed first and secured the other side as more troops continued to follow. The division had succeeded in a second major river crossing in less that twenty-four hours. Rainbow Division was now headed for one of its final objectives: Munich, the birthplace of the Nazi movement.

For the next several days, they continued south. Elements of the 20th Armored Division, along with elements of the 45th Thunderbird Division, were also headed in the same direction toward Munich.

On April 29, 1945, 42nd Infantry Rainbow Division was setting up artillery to fire in the enemy's direction. It was this same day that they happened to stumble upon something they would never forget.

Grandpa suddenly got a solemn look on his face and became quiet as he stared into the stove's flames. We were not sure what to make of it, and sat in silence with him for what seemed like several minutes.

He then took a deep breath and said, "We were on foot as we quietly approached one of the boxcars. It doors had been left open. Our patrol leader motioned for us to come closer. One of my buddies whispered, 'Look at all of that firewood.' We got closer … it was not firewood."

He told us that just outside of Dachau, one of Germany's oldest concentration camps, the Nazis had left about fifty boxcars on the railroad tracks. Inside those boxcars were the bodies of more than a thousand Jews, left to die out in the cold without food or water. He said they had either starved to death or had been murdered by the fleeing Nazis.

"Some looked like they had tried to escape and had been shot," Grandpa said. "What we were actually looking at was a death train filled with dead bodies.

"Inside the concentration camp itself were thousands of prisoners. Many were still alive when our liberating forces arrived, but they had been dying by the hundreds every day.

"This was the real reason why we were fighting. That strange sense of urgency I felt as we arrived in Marseille, France, several months earlier was only confirmed by what I saw."

That was all he would tell us about Dachau. He still had his 42nd Infantry Rainbow Division combat history of World War II book in his hands as he sat there. He got up from where he sat and closed the book. At our age, for the time being, he did not want us to look at the pictures of Dachau that were located inside.

It was getting late, and our parents were calling down to the basement for us. Grandpa gave each of us a hug as we left his wood shop. It would be a few years later before we would learn the full extent of what was recorded in that book and the experiences of Dachau by the men of Rainbow Division. Grandpa was always adamant that what was recorded should never be forgotten.

On April 29, 1945, at 1300 hours, while on their way to Munich, the 222nd Infantry of Rainbow Division stumbled upon Dachau concentration camp, one of the oldest concentration camps in Germany.

A few SS guards who refused to surrender began firing on the approaching American troops. Elements of the 20th Armored Division and 45th Thunderbird Division had also just arrived, and upon learning what was happening, began to attack the camp from the east. The Americans quickly took out the threats. A few SS guards tried to escape into the crowd, disguising themselves in inmate clothes, but were quickly identified by the prisoners and were either beaten to death or killed with their own weapons. As the Americans entered the camp, more than 33,000 prisoners cheered and rushed toward their liberators with arms wide open.

The 42nd and 45th Infantry Division soldiers were soon exposed to sights that filled them with horror. Some fifty boxcars filled with 1,500 dead Jews lined the railroad surrounding the enclosure. They had been left for dead outside the camp without food or water, as there was no room for them in Dachau. Many had also been executed by machine guns.

Inside the camp were dead bodies everywhere. More than 2,000 inmates were killed the night before the arrival of the Americans as the German SS continued its evil, systematic murders. The surviving inmates, starved and beaten, were then ordered to stack the bodies of the dead into piles, as there was no coal to cremate the dead. Since its establishment in 1933, Dachau had executed approximately 200 inmates per day — the majority of whom were stripped of their clothes and marched naked into gas chambers to die.

The men of Rainbow Division would never look at their enemy the same way again. This was the real reason they were fighting. Many of the battle-hardened soldiers broke down as inmates cheered and hugged them, expressing love for their liberators.

Within a few hours of liberation, medical teams moved in to assist the sick and dying. Food supplies were quickly brought in, and the grim work of burying the dead began.

At the same time that Dachau was being liberated, Rainbow Division continued to advance toward its objective: Munich. Once the 222nd Infantry had neutralized the threats at Dachau, it pushed forward toward the Amper River on the outskirts of the city. The 242nd would soon follow, racing down the autobahn.

On April 30, 1945, Rainbow Division 222nd and 242nd Infantry entered Munich and quickly captured the center of the city. The aggressive advance that Rainbow was famous for had again paid off, with the enemy offering no resistance to the overwhelming show of force.

More than 3,000 Germans surrendered and were marched with hands over their heads past areas of the city famous in Nazi history. One such place was the Beer Hall Putsch, where Adolph Hitler had developed oratory skills and delivered some of his first charismatic speeches. He would later become a dictator with the rare gift of motivating the people of Germany into following him in a spirit of mass euphoria and willing blindness.

Grandpa noted that at the same time Rainbow Division was attacking Munich, the Russians were busy moving into Berlin. It was not immediately clear what had happened to Hitler on April 30, 1945. At the time, there were rumors among the troops that he had been buried in the rubble of Berlin. Some said he had been shot. A few said he had committed suicide by cyanide. Others said he had escaped. In the end, all they could gather was that the hope of most of mankind had been realized. Adolf Hitler, leader of the Third Reich — which required a coalition of the world's nations to destroy — had essentially disappeared from the face of the earth.

The German dream for a National Redoubt had been crushed by the men of Rainbow Division. On May 3, the division crossed the Inn River and moved toward the Austrian border.

With no resistance, all that was left to do was continue to search for any of Hitler's remaining SS troops while rounding up German prisoners and moving them to the rear. By May 4, the end of the war in Europe was only a few hours away.

LITTLE BOY AND FAT MAN

```
TOP SECRET

URGENT

WAR 32887

FOR COLONEL KYLE EYES ONLY. FROM HARRISON

FOR MR. STIMSON.

OPERATED ON THIS MORNING. DIAGNOSIS NOT YET

COMPLETE BUT RESULTS SEEM SATISFACTORY AND

ALREADY EXCEED EXPECTATIONS. LOCAL PRESS

RELEASE NECESSARY AS INTERESTS EXTENDS GREAT

DISTANCE. DR. GROVES PLEASED. HE RETURNS

TOMORROW. I WILL KEEP YOU POSTED.
```

(Department of the Army Files: Telegram. The Acting Chairman of the Interim Committee (Harrison) to the Secretary of War (Stimson). Washington, 16 July 1945)

It was a Saturday, and my brothers and I were once again on one of our great adventures. This time we had snuck off from our father, who had taken us with him to church as he practiced piano for the upcoming Sunday service. He was an accomplished pianist. Camp Zion Church was where my grandfather was pastor. It was located just across the road from his home.

We saw Grandpa from across the road tinkering with his red Snapper lawn mower, and we ran over to give him a hug. He was happy to see us and appeared to enjoy taking a break from his mechanical work on the mower. We asked him if he would tell us about how the war ended.

He seemed happy that we remained interested in what he had to say. He still had his tools in his hands as he began where he had left off a few days before.

When the actual surrender of the German army came on May 7, 1945, Grandpa had mentioned that there was little celebration on the part of the men of Rainbow Division. He said they were informed that General Alfred Jodl, who represented the German High Command, signed an unconditional surrender of both the east and west forces in Reims, France. The next day, on May 8, Victory in Europe (VE) Day was declared.

"We had been marching and fighting since March 15. All of us were tired, and most of us just wanted to sleep," he said.

Chaplains held services the day the surrender was announced. There was little celebration, though. The men were anxious about the ongoing war with Japan and worried that, at some point, they could be ordered to go to the Pacific. By May 14, however, they still had their hands full, collecting the thousands of German soldiers who had fled into the Austrian area of Tyrol as well as searching for any remaining members of Hitler's SS — those paramilitary organization members most responsible for the genocidal killing of millions of Jews.

Checkpoints and roadblocks were soon established on

essentially every road leading into the mountainous area. Every vehicle was checked by men of Rainbow Division, and civilians were not allowed to travel outside their hometowns without a pass. Patrols from the division were also dispersed throughout the countryside as a way of checking every house, cabin, and hotel that could possibly be hiding Hitler's SS.

Grandpa told us about one such outing. A Rainbow patrol leader and his men were checking out a lone ski lodge high on a mountaintop. Inside they found and captured, alive, SS General Von Oberg, the "Butcher of Paris."

"A few other SS soldiers were also found hiding in cabins. Another one was killed when he pulled his weapon on an approaching Rainbow soldier," he said.

He also told us that the men of Rainbow Division were sickened by the fact that some of the senior SS officers had escaped and fled the country.

Grandpa noted that they had completed 114 days of combat, which began in the Hardt Mountains of France when they broke through the Westwall of Germany. He said he was very proud that his division had been the first unit in the corps to enter Germany, penetrate the Siegfried Line, cross the Danube, and be first into Munich.

This aggressive offensive attack by Rainbow Division began in the Hardt Mountains of France and continued for approximately 450 miles through hostile enemy German territory until they reached the border of Austria. They had captured the cities of Wurzburg, Schweinfurt, Furth and Munich. Also, Rainbow Division had captured 51,000 prisoners.

Since the German army's surrender, the U.S. had continued to shift more of its focus to the Pacific. Grandpa said that months earlier, at the same time they had been on the attack in Germany, he and the men heard reports about heavy fighting overseas as fellow Americans began storming the beaches of Iwo Jima and Okinawa.

Strategic bombing campaigns had also been underway over the Japanese mainland. On March 9-10, 1945, Tokyo was attacked by approximately 300 U.S. B-29 bomber aircraft carrying incendiary bombs. This firebomb attack killed at least 89,000 and destroyed approximately 250,000 buildings, leaving one million people homeless.

As the war in Germany came to a close, Grandpa said that a training program was instituted to begin preparing the men of Rainbow Division for their expected deployment to the Pacific.

"After having made it through Germany, I was lucky to still be alive," he said. "Now I would have to make it through an invasion into Japan, halfway across the world, in order to get back home to my wife and children. It seemed impossible, and I had a deep feeling of despair."

American planners were already focusing on an invasion of the Japanese islands of Kyushu and Honshu, known as Operation Downfall. There was also talk that the Russians, who had successfully fought their way through the Eastern Front of Germany, could likely cooperate with the Americans to end the war in the Pacific. There were no signs of Japan surrendering anytime soon, and an invasion would likely result in a very high number of American casualties. Grandpa said America also feared that if

Russia did get involved, its leaders would demand a share in the occupation of Japan, just as they were doing in Europe.

Back home in Virginia, Alma and the children again gathered around the radio, listening for any information as to when Blace and the men of Rainbow Division might return home. They were unaware of the redeployment training program for the Pacific, but Alma could read between the lines as the radio broadcast a speech by President Truman on June 7, 1945:

There can be no peace in the world until the military power of Japan is destroyed with the same completeness as was the power of the European dictators. To do that, we are now engaged in a process of deploying millions of our armed forces against Japan in a mass movement of troops and supplies and weapons over 14,000 miles, a military and naval feat unequal in all history. Substantial portions of Japan's key industrial centers have been leveled to the ground in a series a record incendiary raids. What has already happened to Tokyo will happen to every Japanese city whose industries feed the Japanese war machine. If the Japanese insist on continuing resistance, beyond the point of reason, their country will suffer the same destruction as Germany. Our blows will destroy their whole modern industrial plant and organization, which they have built up during the past century and which they are now devoting to a hopeless cause. We have no desire or intention to destroy or enslave the Japanese people, but only surrender can prevent the kind of ruin which they have seen come to Germany as a result of continued useless resistance.

Grandpa said that in July the 42nd Division received orders to move to the vicinity of Salzburg, Austria, and that the French were to take over the occupation of Tyrol. The men of Rainbow Division were ordered to begin eight weeks of redeployment training for the Pacific, as required by the Third Army.

"We were kept busy with occupation duty," he said. "We also continued training for the Pacific theater, learning all we could about the Japanese Army and their war tactics."

He told us that the men had heard reports that President Truman had arrived in Germany, near Berlin, and was to hold meetings with British Prime Minister Winston Churchill and Soviet leader Joseph Stalin. It was to be called the Berlin Meeting, but Berlin had been so heavily damaged that the meeting was moved by the Russians to Potsdam. Known as the Potsdam Conference, the meetings were to negotiate terms for the future of Germany and postwar Europe. This would eventually lead to the Potsdam Agreement between America, Great Britain, and the Soviet Union regarding the military occupation and reconstruction of Germany and the entire European theater.

"We didn't have time to celebrate when the Germans surrendered," Grandpa said. "We were turning our attention to Japan. President Roosevelt had previously insisted on the unconditional surrender of the Japanese, and President Truman continued with that demand after Roosevelt's death. The conflict in Europe was only half of the second world war. To us, the end of the war with Japan seemed a long way off."

What Grandpa and the men of Rainbow Division didn't know at the time was that an American effort, which began in

1941, had been secretly underway to design and build the first atomic bomb. This effort was known as the Manhattan Project.

Four years after the start of the Manhattan Project, President Truman was handed a specific top secret telegram from Secretary of War Stimson a few days after his arrival in the Berlin suburb of Babelsberg:

```
TOP SECRET
URGENT
WAR 32887
FOR COLONEL KYLE EYES ONLY. FROM HARRISON
FOR MR. STIMSON.
OPERATED ON THIS MORNING. DIAGNOSIS NOT YET
COMPLETE BUT RESULTS SEEM SATISFACTORY AND
ALREADY EXCEED EXPECTATIONS. LOCAL PRESS
RELEASE NECESSARY AS INTERESTS EXTENDS GREAT
DISTANCE. DR. GROVES PLEASED. HE RETURNS
TOMORROW. I WILL KEEP YOU POSTED.
```

This was a top secret telegram from the acting chairman of the Interim Committee (Harrison) to the Secretary of War (Stimson) dated July 16, 1945. It was the first word received from Washington regarding the successful test of the atomic bomb in New Mexico.

A few days later, while still in Germany, President Truman received a detailed report on the atomic explosion at Alamogordo Air Base, New Mexico. It was prepared by Major General Groves and his second-in command, Brigadier General Thomas F. Farrell:

1. This is not a concise, formal military report but an attempt to recite what I would have told you if you had been here on my return from New Mexico.

2. At 0530, 16 July 1945, in a remote section of the Alamogordo Air Base, New Mexico, the first full scale test was made of the implosion type atomic fission bomb. For the first time in history there was a nuclear explosion. And what an explosion! The bomb was not dropped from an airplane but was exploded on a platform on top of a 100-foot high steel tower.

3. The test was successful beyond the most optimistic expectations of anyone. Based on the data which it has been possible to work up to date, I estimate the energy generated to be in excess of the equivalent of 15,000 to 20,000 tons of TNT; and this is a conservative estimate. Data based on measurements which we have not been able to reconcile would make the energy release several times the conservative figure. There were tremendous blast effects. For a brief period, there was a lighting effect within a radius of 20 miles equal to several suns in mid-day; a huge ball of fire was formed which lasted for several seconds. This ball mushroomed and rose to a height of over 10,000 feet before it dimmed. The light from the explosion was seen clearly at Albuquerque, Santa Fe, Silver City, El Paso and other points generally to about 180 miles away. The sound was heard to the same distance in a few instances but generally to about 100 miles away. Only a few windows were broken although one was some 125 miles away.

With the development of the atomic bomb, the United States would not need Russian participation in the war against Japan. Plans were already underway for its potential use in the Pacific.

Later that month, on July 26, the cruiser Indianapolis arrived at Tinian Island in the Pacific with its top secret cargo delivery for the 509th Composite Air Group: the uranium-235 portion of the atomic bomb. That same day, the United States, Great Britain, and China released the Potsdam Declaration, detailing the terms for Japan's surrender. It stated flatly that if Japan did not surrender, it would face "prompt and utter destruction."

Japan's prime minister responded to the declaration with defiance: "I consider the joint proclamation of the three powers to be a rehash of the Cairo Declaration. The government does not regard it as a thing of great value; the government will just ignore it. We will press forward resolutely to carry the war to a successful conclusion."

On August 1, thousands of leaflets, known as the LeMay bombing leaflets, were dropped over Japan's major cities by approximately one hundred American B-29 bombers. These leaflets warned the Japanese civilians of the necessity of surrender.

The Japanese army had rejected the Postman Declaration and ignored its ominous warnings. On August 6, 1945, a Boeing B-29 Superfortress bomber, the Enola Gay, took off from Tinian Island. At 8:15 a.m., it dropped the first atomic bomb, nicknamed Little Boy, on the city of Hiroshima. President Truman would later acknowledge the United States' possession of the atomic bomb:

> The world will note that the first atomic bomb was dropped on
> Hiroshima, a military base. That was because we wished in this first

attack to avoid, insofar as much as possible, the killing of civilians. But that attack is only a warning of things to come. If Japan does not surrender, bombs will have to be dropped on her war industries and, unfortunately, thousands of civilian lives will be lost. I urge Japanese civilians to leave industrial cities immediately, and save themselves from destruction.

Having found the bomb, we have used it. We have used it against those who attacked us without warning at Pearl Harbor, against those who have starved and beaten and executed American prisoners of war, against those who have abandoned all pretense of obeying international laws of warfare. We have used it in order to shorten the agony of war, in order to save the lives of thousands and thousands of young Americans.

President Truman again called for Japan's surrender and warned them to "expect a rain of ruin from the air, the like of which has never been seen on this earth." On August 9, 1945, three days after the bombing of Hiroshima, another atomic strike was carried out when another B-29, named Bockscar, dropped the atomic bomb nicknamed Fat Man on the city of Nagasaki.

Following these bombings, Japanese Emperor Hirohito ordered the Supreme Council for the Direction of the War to accept the terms the Allies had demanded in the Potsdam Declaration. On August 15, 1945, Emperor Hirohito announced Japan's termination of war in a recorded radio address known as the Jewel Voice Broadcast. The surrender of Japan was formally signed on September 2, 1945, aboard the battleship USS Missouri, bringing a close to the second world war.

The war with Japan was now over. Grandpa said he breathed a sigh of relief, knowing he would not be headed to the Pacific. The men of Rainbow Division realized that with Japan's surrender, they would likely stay in Europe for a while and be a part of an occupation force in Austria. But they also knew Japan's surrender meant that they could possibly be heading home soon — which could not come quick enough.

Many soldiers were now occupied with the points system — a way the military figured out who got to go home first. The more points you had earned, the quicker you would be returning home. This was calculated, for example, by the number of battles you were in, medals earned, time spent in service as well as overseas, and even points for dependent children under the age of eighteen.

By September, some of the men had already began leaving the division for home. At the same time, new troops were arriving in Europe, taking the place of veterans returning home. The new arrivals would also become Rainbow soldiers and play a major role in keeping the peace.

Grandpa reminded us that Germany had formally surrendered on May 7, 1945, and that 42nd Rainbow Division had been busy with its part in the joint occupation of Germany as well as training for their expected deployment to the Pacific. The atomic bomb changed all that, and Japan formally surrendered on September 2. Even with the points system, it would be another three months of occupation duty in Germany before Blace would return to the United States.

Replacement troops continued to arrive, and the day finally came for Blace and a few of the remaining men he had fought with to pack their duffle bags in preparation for the first part of their journey home. It had been an aggressive, hard-fought battle through Germany, which none of the survivors would ever forget.

The war was fought mostly through the mud and rubble of destroyed cities, but the scenery before them now was the complete opposite. The men found themselves surrounded by the towering, beautiful, majestic mountains of the Alps. Lush, green valleys with chains of mountain peaks tipped with snow covered the distant horizon. As far as the eye could see, beautiful chalets were carved into the hillsides. Meadow creeks and brawling white-water streams flowed from above, leading down into crystal-clear lakes. These fast moving streams and creeks were known for their brown and brook trout, and seemed to beg for someone to come and fish.

Grandpa and the men paused and looked at one another as if to see who would be the first to break rank and go fishing. Then broke out in laughter. It was the first time in many months any of the men had laughed.

"All thoughts were of home," he said. "We couldn't wait to get back home."

Epilogue

I'll always cherish the time I spent listening to my grandfather's war story. For me and my brothers and cousins, it was a rare opportunity to gain firsthand insight into what he had went through — not only as a soldier in the 42nd Rainbow Division, but also as a husband and father.

In the years following the war, he was not known for his time in the military, as he rarely ever told anyone that he had been in the Army. Upon his return home, he quickly resumed his construction job and tried as best he could to put the memories of war behind him. If it were not for my older brother, Eddie, who asked him to tell us about the war, I do not think any of us would have known the full extent of what Grandpa experienced. Further insight into what he had been through was captured on an audiotape recorded by a family member years later. Grandpa was very generous in allowing us to look back with him at a short but very important time in his life, those years of 1944 and 1945.

The war changed him, as it would change anyone who went through combat — but especially someone who had witnessed the horrific Dachau concentration camp. He, along with the men of 42nd Rainbow Division, saw the results of the Nazis' "evil" deeds in their most grotesque form. They did not want to live in a world where evil prevailed.

Rainbow Division unexpectedly took part in the liberation of Dachau concentration camp on April 29, 1945. Grandpa would carry the memories of Dachau for the remainder of his life. Likewise, what he shared with us, we will never forget.

For months following the end of the war, prominent members of Nazi Germany were brought to trial in Nuremberg. They were eventually found guilty and convicted of war crimes.

Blace had never gotten over having to leave behind his wife, Alma, and their children when he got drafted. He could only imagine the worry and sleepless nights he had caused his family during those war years. He planned on spending the remainder of his life trying, in some way, to make it right.

His oldest son, Richard, in a letter he wrote to one of his sisters, recalled what it was like when the war ended: "The day the war ended, celebrations began. Chap Rector, Eldean, and I drove to downtown Galax and joined in the horn blowing, flag waving and merriment. It was very crowded and noisy. I had never seen so many happy people."

For weeks after the end of the war, Blace's children were constantly asking their mother if she had heard of any news of when their father would get to come home. No one knew how long his part in the joint occupation of Germany would be. Each night, they prayed for his safe return.

A few months later, Richard, just nine days shy of his eleventh birthday, was walking home alone on Poplar Grove Road. He was returning from Gene Cooley's grocery store when he heard a car coming up from behind him on the old dusty dirt road. The car passed by but then suddenly stopped in the middle of the road.

Through the dust he could see that it was a taxi, and a man was running from the vehicle toward him with arms wide open. It was his father.

Richard dropped what he was carrying and ran to his father. They met together in a tight embrace. It had been a long separation. Richard's prayers for his father's safe return had been answered. With their arms still locked in embrace, he joined his dad as they headed toward home.

At home, Alma had just put the finishing touches on her yellow cake with seven-minute frosting. She was placing the cake inside her china hutch when she saw her three oldest daughters, Joanne, Blenda, and Helen, running to the front window to look outside.

"It's Dad!" they screamed.

Alma was overcome with emotion as she watched her children run out to meet their father.

Blace was seeing his children for the first time in more than a year, and he was surprised how much they had grown and changed.

Inside the house, while holding little Eddie (Janie and Judy were older, too, but still toddlers, and were playing inside), Alma waited as Blace made his way to the front door. With tears flowing, no words were needed as Blace and Alma embraced. It was a time of celebration.

The war had tried its best to separate the family. Only with God's help would the family make it through Blace's transition from the military back to society as a father and husband.

There were also the mental and emotional effects of war to

deal with. Post-traumatic stress was all too common for soldiers returning home after the terrifying and life-threatening experiences of combat. In that day, little was known about it. There would be many sleepless nights filled with anxiety, flashbacks, and nightmares. It would take a while for the household to return to normal, but God was still at work.

Slowly, Blace continued his transition from soldier back to civilian, but something was still amiss.

In the early 1950s, Blace and Alma heard about a large gospel tent meeting near their home, where the Rev. H. Richard Hall was holding a revival. They decided to attend the service. While listening to the message, Blace could not help but recall all the many times his life had been spared during the war. He thought back to how his troop ship had made it safely through the stormy sea on its way to Europe … how it just so happened that a member of the 45th Infantry Division had been at the right place at the right time and stopped Blace and his battle buddy from knocking a picture of Hitler off the wall — a picture that was wired with explosives … how he had survived an exploding artillery shell that should have killed him, leaving him briefly unconscious with shrapnel wounds to his face and neck. He was also reminded of the time he was pinned down under the fire of several automatic weapons — yet never hit — as he and Steller tried to outflank a machine gun nest … how, under direct enemy fire, he had moved out onto a bridge over the Lech River in the darkness of night and begun repairing the structure even though many of the combat engineers around him were shot and wounded in the process.

Yes, he had witnessed war firsthand and seen it take the lives of many men, but somehow he had survived. There, in the gospel tent meeting, he realized that God had to have been with him and seen him through the war. There was no other explanation for his survival. God had a plan for sparing his life. When the invitation was given, he walked forward along the sawdust floor and renewed his commitment to the Lord.

"That day changed my life forever," he said.

To the surprise of his family, he later became an ordained minister. He would spend the remainder of his life sharing the gospel through the foothills of Virginia and in later years as senior pastor of Camp Zion Church in Galax, Virginia.

It was after that tent meeting that Alma could see a change in her husband. "He's different," she said. "He's different."

After witnessing a change in her husband over the next several months, she began to take note of her own life. Shortly after, on July 10, 1954, kneeling in the upstairs room of their Poplar Grove home, Alma prayed the following prayer: "I don't know what he has, but whatever it is, Lord I want it. He's different."

Their daughter Judy, who was only ten years old at that time, later documented in the back of an old family Bible the following: "Mom's answer to her prayer when she was converted July 10, 1954." "But verily God hath heard me; he hath attended to the voice of my prayer." (Psalm 66:19, King James Version).

On May 23, 1960, thoughts of the war must have resurfaced for Blace when he and the world heard the news of the capture of the infamous Nazi SS officer Adolf Eichmann in Argentina by Israeli undercover agents. During the war, Eichmann was appointed to carry out the extermination of Europe's Jewish population by sending millions of Jews from occupied Europe to Nazi death camps, where they met their end in gas chambers or were worked to death.

On April 11, 1961, Eichmann's trial began in Jerusalem. It was televised to the world. He was hanged for his war crimes against the Jewish people on May 31, 1962.

As the war years faded to a distant memory, Blace continued to press on. He had done what he could during that part of his life and was still working to make the world a better place as a minister of the gospel.

Through it all, my grandparents remained committed to their marriage, which lasted for more than 50 years. My grandfather retired from the ministry in 1989.

I think what Grandpa would have most wanted for all of us was to always remember — to look back and never forget. Sure, we were only teenagers when he first told us his war story, but I think he knew that as we grew older, each of us would have the opportunity at some point to look back and reflect on our own lives. In doing so, maybe we too could catch a glimpse of how God had brought us through the twists and turns of life. I am sure he would agree that this would only help to build our faith — realizing that God abides with us, even in the troubles and heartaches of life.

"God never promised to keep us from the storms of life," he used to say, "but promised to be with us through the storms of life."

Grandpa also taught us that, when faced with adversity and when things look their darkest, God always leaves a remnant.

Just when the Germans were thinking they were about to achieve the Final Solution — a plan for the extermination of all Jews — Grandpa witnessed firsthand a remnant that survived Dachau, a people who would have their own Jewish state just three years later, on May 14, 1948.

Prior to their deaths, my grandfather, along with his wife and siblings, made one last trip back to the mountains of Kentucky. It had been more than sixty years since he had been back to the place that so tragically had taken the life of his little brother. Grandpa said he always had hope of one day bringing the remains of his little brother Kelly back from those mountains to be interred beside his mother and father. Grandpa's father, J.E., was tragically injured when he fell from the roof of his home in Virginia, striking his head on a cement sidewalk below. He died a few days later, in Roanoke, on February 15, 1959. His wife, Vera, would survive him until her death on February 14, 1975.

The landscape in Kentucky had changed drastically. Where there used to be open fields, there now was a thick overgrowth of kudzu. My grandmother said it was one of the snakiest areas she had ever seen. The old Kentucky homestead had gone to ruin long, long before. What was left of its location was marked only by few pieces of logs and some foundation stones. The family thought they had located the area near some railroad tracks where Kelly had been laid to rest, but the piece of rock used for a headstone, marked with the initials "K.D.," was never found. The actual location of Kelly's final resting place remains a mystery to this day.

My grandfather was a man of faith. He never lost his trust in his Lord and Savior, and he looked forward to one day being reunited with his little brother. On November 2, 1991, he did just that, in the intensive care unit of Twin County Community Hospital, with his wife, sons and daughters by his bedside.

I'll never forget him.

BIBLIOGRAPHY

Butler, Rupert. *The Black Angels*. New York: St Martin's Press. 1979.

"Camp Devens Letter." British Medical Journal, 22 December 1979; Vol 2, issue 1632.

Cavendish, Marshall. *The Marshall Cavendish Illustrated Encyclopedia of World War II: An Objective, Chronological, and Comprehensive History of the Second World War.* Marshall Cavendish. New York. 1972.

Cole, Hugh M. *The Ardennes: The Battle of the Bulge.* Washington, D.C.: Office of the Chief of Military History, 1965.

Daly, Hugh C. and United States Army. *42nd "Rainbow" Infantry Division: A Combat History of World War II.* Army & Navy Publishing Company. Baton Rouge, Louisiana. 1946.

Davis, Blace. Audio Cassette Family Interview, May 8, 1985.

Davis, Richard. Letter to Nancy, 23 September 1998. The original letter is in the possession of Nancy Wiseman, Ocala, Florida. Letter used with permission.

Department of the Army Files: Telegram. The Acting Chairman of the Interim Committee (Harrison) to the Secretary of War (Stimson). Washington, 16 July 1945.

Honor: WWII Veterans Statistics. The National WWII Museum | New Orleans. http://www.nationalww2museum.org (accessed October 12, 2017).

"Kristallnacht." United States Holocaust Memorial Museum. https://www.ushmm.org/ (accessed May 15, 2017).

Lutzer, Erwin W. *When A Nation Forgets God: 7 Lessons We Must Learn From Nazi Germany.* Moody Publishers. 2010

"Manhattan Project." Atomic Heritage Foundation. http://www.atomicheritage.org/ (accessed May 15, 2017).

Williams, Josette H. "The Information War in the Pacific, 1945." CIA Studies in Intelligence. Vol. 46, NO. 3, 2002 Unclassified Edition. https://www.cia.gov/library/center-for-the-study-of-intelligence/csi-publications/csi-studies/studies/vol46no3/article07.html (accessed May 15, 2017).

Pillbox Warfare in the Siegfried Line. Intelligence Bulletin MILITARY INTELLIGENCE DIVISION War Department Washington 25, D.C. Vol. III, No. 5: January 1945.

President Truman Warns Japanese to Give Up. https://archive.org/details/1945-06-07_Pres_Truman_Warns_Japs_To_Give_Up (accessed May 15, 2017).

Radio Report to the American People on the Potsdam Conference, August 9, 1945. Harry S. Truman Library & Museum. https://www.trumanlibrary.org/publicpapers/?pid=104 (accessed May 15, 2017).

The Holy Bible, King James Version. Cambridge Edition: 1769; King James Bible Online, 2017. http://www.kingjamesbibleonline.org./ (accessed May 15, 2017).

Truman, Margaret. *Harry S. Truman.* William Morrow and Co. (1973). Memoir by his daughter. pp. 268-276.

U.S. Army Awards of the Silver Star. http://www.homeofheroes.com/members/04_SS/2_WWII/indexes/army/Army-W.html (accessed May 15, 2017).

Westwall Museum Irrel- http://www.westwallmuseum-irrel.de/ (accessed May 15, 2017).

Wikipedia contributors, "Bombing of Tokyo," Wikipedia, The Free Encyclopedia, https://en.wikipedia.org/w/index.php?title=Bombing_of_Tokyo&oldid=776234291 (accessed May 15, 2017).

Wikipedia contributors, "Bombing of Würzburg in World War II," Wikipedia, The Free Encyclopedia, https://en.wikipedia.org/w/index.php?title=Bombing_of_W%C3%BCrzburg_in_World_War_II&oldid=776030179 (accessed May 15, 2017).

Wikipedia contributors, "42nd Infantry Division (United States)," Wikipedia, The
   Free Encyclopedia, https://en.wikipedia.org/w/index.php?title=42nd_Infantry_
   Division_(United_States)&oldid=779744788 (accessed May 15, 2017).

Wikipedia contributors, "45th Infantry Division (United States)," Wikipedia, The
   Free Encyclopedia, https://en.wikipedia.org/w/index.php?title=45th_Infantry_
   Division_(United_States)&oldid=779459494 (accessed May 15, 2017).

Wikipedia contributors, "Jewel Voice Broadcast," Wikipedia, The Free
   Encyclopedia, https://en.wikipedia.org/w/index.php?title=Jewel_Voice_
   Broadcast&oldid=778793138 (accessed May 15, 2017).

Wikipedia contributors, "Nuremberg Rally," Wikipedia, The Free
   Encyclopedia, https://en.wikipedia.org/w/index.php?title=Nuremberg_
   Rally&oldid=779252558 (accessed May 15, 2017).

Wikipedia contributors, "Operation Downfall," Wikipedia, The Free
   Encyclopedia, https://en.wikipedia.org/w/index.php?title=Operation_
   Downfall&oldid=780566473 (accessed May 15, 2017).

Wikipedia contributors, "Operation Nordwind," Wikipedia, The Free
   Encyclopedia, https://en.wikipedia.org/w/index.php?title=Operation_
   Nordwind&oldid=778885994 (accessed May 15, 2017).

Wikipedia contributors, "Second Raid on Schweinfurt," Wikipedia, The Free
   Encyclopedia, https://en.wikipedia.org/w/index.php?title=Second_Raid_on_
   Schweinfurt&oldid=779085519 (accessed May 15, 2017).

Yad Vashem: The World Holocaust Remembrance Center. http://www1.yadvashem.
   org/yv/en/holocaust/resource_center/index.asp (accessed May 15, 2017).

ABOUT THE AUTHOR

Mark A. Davis received his degree in physician assistant studies from Jefferson College of Health Sciences in Roanoke, Virginia, in 2004. He has lived most of his life in the foothills of Virginia. He is a veteran of the United States armed forces and has practiced medicine as a physician assistant for the Department of the Army, taking part in the treatment and care of active duty service members, veterans, and their families. He currently resides in South Carolina with his wife, Melissa.

www.ingramcontent.com/pod-product-compliance
Lightning Source LLC
LaVergne TN
LVHW051642080426

835511LV00016B/2445